THE
MONEY
IS THE
GRAVY

THE
MONEY
IS THE
GRAVY

Finding the Career
That Nourishes You

JOHN CLARK

WARNER BOOKS

An AOL Time Warner Company

This book was originally published in New Zealand by Tandem Press and in the UK by Random House/Century UK under the title *The Money or Your Life*.

Warner Books, Inc., 1271 Avenue of the Americas, New York, NY 10020
Visit our Web site at www.twbookmark.com

 An AOL Time Warner Company

Printed in the United States of America

First Printing: March 2003

10   9   8   7   6   5   4   3   2   1

Library of Congress Cataloging-in-Publication Data

Clark, John Douglas,
    The money is the gravy : finding the career that nourishes you /
    John Clark.
        p. cm.
    Originally published: The money or your life. [New Zealand] :
    Tandem Press, 1997.
    ISBN 0-446-52918-4
    1. Job satisfaction. 2. Self-actualization (Psychology) I. Title.

HF5549.5.J63 C5837 2003
650'.14—dc21
                                                        2002027228

Book design/text composition HRoberts Design

To Jude, Megan, and Andrew

Acknowledgments

When Peter Sutherland suggested a decade ago that I write a book, the idea struck me as preposterous. But he is nothing if not persistent. Having sown the seed in arid soil, he watered it assiduously until, eventually, it sprouted. I am profoundly grateful to him and Ainslie for all their encouragement.

I thank Crystal Beavis, Hugh Caughley, Belinda Cordwell, Libby Gemmell, Liz Gunn, Alasdair Hardman, Philip Harkness, John Hart, Ken Johnston, David Patterson, Judith Saunders, Melanie Tollemache, Doreen Wilson, and the many others who have provided practical and moral support.

I cannot speak too highly of my agent, Brian DeFiore. It cannot be easy, Brian, to act for an author you've never met, one who talks with a funny accent and live on the other side of the globe. Your staunch belief the book and your dedication to seeing it published in the United States have been an inspiration.

Similarly, I have been blessed by the wonderful support of many folks at Warner Books. I couldn't have asked for more from my editor, Amy Einhorn. She and Sandra Bark were hugely enthusiastic, committed, and attentive at all times. Others too numerous to mention contributed mightily to the production and launch effort. My thanks go to you all for your energy, creativity, and care, as well as your expertise.

This book had its first incarnation in New Zealand some years ago. I shall always be indebted to Bob Ross of Tandem Press for serving as the midwife.

Montaigne wrote once that "in this book I have only made up a bunch of other people's flowers, and that of my own I have only provided the string that binds them together." That is precisely how I feel. There is nothing new in this book. I have simply borrowed ideas from others much wiser than I. The bibliography lists some of the many authors who have influenced me. Three stand out: Joseph Campbell, whose "follow your bliss" tenet resonated with me at a time when I was struggling to find a focus; Charles Handy, who has provided counsel as well as inspiration; and Jon Kabat-Zinn, who has helped me learn how to "be here now."

Most of all, I thank my wife, Jude. Her support, in ways too many to mention, has been extraordinary. In particular, she has borne the brunt of looking after our two young children during the writing of this book. Conscious that at times family commitments have threatened publishing deadlines, she once suggested facetiously that I dedicate the book to my family "despite whom this book was written." The truth is, of course, that it is Jude who has made the book possible.

Contents

Introduction

Once upon a time, more than fifteen years ago, I was a commercial lawyer. (It would be wrong to say that this was my *chosen* career; I simply stood mindlessly on a conveyor belt that took me from high school to law school to legal practice.) To the world I presented the veneer of an "achiever." I had a New Zealand honors degree and a U.S. master's degree. I had practiced law in New Zealand, London, and Detroit. I was the managing partner of a prominent law firm. I had a large base of loyal clients, an expanding profile, and a high income. That was the me that the world saw: the *external* me.

For many of my colleagues, the practice of law was a vocation. For me, however, it was just a career. And so there existed a gulf between the external me and the inner me. Inside I felt as though I had achieved nothing of value. I felt anxious, lonely, insecure, weary. I had a vague sense that I—the *real* me—was someone different from the person who was playing the various roles the world saw and judged. Not that I had any idea who the real me was. I simply sensed that, whoever it was, I violated it every day that I remained a lawyer.

Admittedly, lawyering had its satisfactions. I liked and respected my colleagues and clients. I found it rewarding to develop staff and work in teams. On occasion I would become absorbed in the intellectual challenge of solving legal problems. And of course there were external trappings, in the form of money, prestige, recognition, and the esteem of others.

Those trappings seemed important to me then; I needed them as props. But they failed to give me an *inner* sense of well-being and security. As the years passed, a sense of emptiness, even deadness, grew within me. It was as if my core were shriveling up and dying.

I assumed then that career angst was an isolated phenomenon confined to me and a few other unfortunates. I was wrong. It is rife throughout the world of managers and professionals—in the United States, Canada, and in fact all the developed economies. It distresses me to come across, each and every day, extraordinary individuals who are engaged (usually very "successfully") in work that they do not value and that uses only a fraction of their talents. Such people feel empty and insecure, though their work achievements may be judged glittering by others.

What makes it worse is that this pain is avoidable. The world of work is changing dramatically. Generations past had little choice but to accept the monolithic model of a lifetime career—something to be chosen in young adulthood and persevered with until retirement forty-five years later. Now there exists an abundance of choice. In the twenty-first century, the scope for tailoring work to the person will grow still further. Those who arm themselves with the mind-set and skills needed to take advantage of this new flexibility have the chance to build fulfilling and secure working lives. For those who don't, protection from the buffeting winds of change will be ever harder to find.

Career orthodoxy, unfortunately, is stuck in a time warp and ignores the new choices. If you subscribe to this orthodoxy (it is hard not to—it is drummed into most of us from an early age):

- You see work as a distinct, and relatively static, compartment of your life. It coexists uneasily with—and usually dominates—other compartments.
- You work to satisfy an economic purpose: earning a living.
- You regard work as the opposite of leisure. Leisure is voluntary and enjoyable. Work is mandatory; any enjoyment is a bonus. As J. M. Barrie put it, "It is not real work unless you would rather be doing something else."

These attitudes were understandable one hundred, fifty, even twenty-five years ago. It is time now to discard them.

The Money Is the Gravy contrasts the concept of "career"—with its sterile connotations of money, status, and duty—with the concept of "calling." If you are pursuing your calling, you are, in Joseph Campbell's powerful phrase, "following your bliss":

- Your work is a freely chosen, life-enhancing activity, integrated with all the other threads of your life.
- You work to fulfill a biological purpose: personal growth and self-expression.
- Your work is a form of leisure, and inherently enjoyable.

Each of these orientations has its pros and cons. If you choose to travel along the orthodox career path, the bad news is that you are likely to experience a life of angst, including a debilitating sense of talents wasted, opportunities lost, a life unlived. The good news is that you can expect to be well rewarded financially. You will have, moreover, plenty of company, for this is the path that all too many well-educated people select.

If you choose to find and pursue your calling, the bad news is that your lifestyle may need to be less splendid. The good news is that you will enjoy a rich, vital, full life. You will be far more secure than all those poor folk with a fine bank balance but a shriveled sense of self.

It's your choice. Which are you going to choose? The money or your life?

Twenty years ago, I chose the money. Back then, I was stuck in orthodox career mode. I would have dismissed as romantic rubbish Bette Davis's concept of a calling: "To fulfill a dream, to be allowed to sweat over lonely labor, to be given a chance to create, is the meat and potatoes of life. The money is the gravy."

Since then, however, I have been on a journey. It has taken me, so far, from legal practice into general management, then on into a fulfilling mix of consulting, teaching, writing, mentoring, study, and voluntary work. Above all, it has been, and continues to be, a journey of self-discovery.

One of the things I have learned is that, yes, money *is* just the gravy.

These days I love my work. There was a time when it seemed to me foolish to even hope for such a thing. I now know that it is a proper and realistic goal—one that you, too, can realize if you adopt the mind-set of an explorer and set off today to find your calling.

The Stakes

"So this is hell. Why, it looks just like my old office!"

ONE

Angst

Both success and failure are difficult to endure. Along with success come drugs, divorce, fornication, bullying, travel, meditation, medication, depression, neurosis and suicide. With failure comes failure.

JOSEPH HELLER

THE BIG LIE

"Go west, young man," they said a century ago. Today, they say, to young men and women alike, "Go find a career."

They say, or slyly imply, that a career will bring health, wealth, and happiness. But it's a con. Careers may well bring wealth, but all too often they harm health and lock out happiness.

What careers most often bring is angst. They should come with a government warning: CAREERS CAN BE HAZARDOUS TO YOUR HEALTH.

You think I'm exaggerating? Sadly, the angst-ridden achievers described in the next few pages are not abnormal. They and their like abound in every career you can name.

Emptiness, Weariness: Maggie, 31, Accountant

Maggie has finally made it. She has just become a partner in an international accounting firm. It is for this that she has striven so hard over the past eight years. And it *has* been hard. There was a time when accountants simply had to process and bill the work that came in the door. Now to become a partner in the firm, Maggie has had to prove that she could develop staff, build new business, manage client relationships, plus meet a huge fees budget. On top of all that she has had an infant daughter to look after. Little wonder that over the last three years she has usually ended up back at the office after dinner.

For years the goal in front of her has been to become a partner. Yet the expected feeling of triumph is lacking. A line from a Peggy Lee song keeps running through her head: *Is that all there is?* Her goal having been achieved, it now seems empty, worthless. Indeed, her whole working life seems empty. Which, she tells herself, is absurd—how can it be empty when at the same time it is too busy, too full?

> Need and struggle are what excite and inspire us; our hour of triumph is what brings the void.
>
> *William James*

In those all-too-few hours that Maggie spends relaxing with her husband and daughter, it often strikes her that Maggie-the-accountant is an adopted persona, a facade that she presents to the world. But if that is so, who is the real Maggie inside the facade? There she draws a blank. Inside the facade is—nothing. *Hello,* she feels like shouting, *is anyone in there?*

For the last few years Maggie has been constantly, numbingly weary. Nothing seems to help: not sleep, not vacations, not vitamin tablets, not exercise. She tells herself that this simply reflects an overbusy life. But often she finds herself thinking that both the weariness and the busy-ness are rooted in her feeling of emptiness, and that this in turn has something to do with her career choice. This thought is unwelcome; she banishes it. Or tries to; but like a boomerang, it keeps returning.

Bitterness, Isolation: Phil, 45, Banker

Most would judge Phil's career to have been successful. He heads one of the three divisions of a major bank, reporting directly to the CEO. But he feels that he has failed. Two years ago he was overlooked for the top job; now he suspects that it will never come his way.

Phil buries himself in his work. He grumbles bitterly to his long-suffering wife, Emily, about the demands placed on him. He tells her that the new CEO is "not up to it" and relies on Phil to keep him out of trouble. And he complains that his own senior staff verge on the incompetent.

Emily is Phil's second wife. He has two children by his first marriage but doesn't see much of them, even though they live with their mother only ten minutes away. When they were young, he seldom arrived home before they were in bed. As they grew older, he took a perfunctory interest in their sports and grudgingly helped with their homework on occasions. They are now at college; his part in their lives is largely confined to writing out checks.

The bank is a convenient scapegoat for everything that is not working in Phil's life. He likes to portray it as Darth Vader, a malevolent being that has sucked him dry, devoured his energies, poisoned his relationships, and cast its evil shadow over the whole of his life.

Yet on and on he toils, deriving little inner nourishment from his work, increasingly estranged from family and isolated from colleagues, drinking too much, declining to take vacations due to him, and desperately clinging to the idea of his own indispensability.

Insecurity: Joanna, 42, Director of Marketing

Joanna's friends call her Wonder Woman. She has been married to Bill, a chemical engineer, for nineteen years. In the first nine of those years, she raised three children almost single-handedly, twice supervised the con-

> Human beings, as far as I can tell, seem to be divided into two subspecies—the resigned, who live in quiet desperation, and the exhausted, who live in restless agitation.
>
> *Sarah Ban Breathnach*

> You can be the head of a large company, you can be the center of your world, and still feel very isolated. By isolation I mean not feeling a real sense of intimate connection with other people. Many people with a lot of friends and family will say to themselves, "There are parts of me that no one really knows—and if they did know, then they'd be out of here, they'd leave me."
>
> *Dean Ornish*

struction of new family homes, organized four stunningly successful fund-raising drives for local charities, and served on the town council. At age twenty-eight, she began part-time study for a marketing degree, which she completed five years later. She now heads the marketing team in a national retail chain.

Friends, colleagues, people in the community, all see Joanna as achievement and success personified. But secretly she suffers from a profound sense of inadequacy. Often a wave of despair from deep within overwhelms her, a feeling of utter worthlessness. At such times she finds it hard to acknowledge that she has any strengths at all. She sees herself as a complex of ugly weaknesses: an incompetent marketer, an inept manager of staff, a lousy wife and mother. *Sooner or later,* she thinks, *I'll be exposed for what I am: an impostor, a fraud undeserving of the accolades bestowed on me.*

Entrapment, Grayness: David, 48, Civil Servant

David's career in the public service has brought him prestige, influence, recognition, and significant financial rewards. Outwardly he is successful. But inwardly he feels hopelessly ensnared in a dense thicket of obligations. At work, colleagues, politicians, staff, other government agencies, and the media make unceasing demands on him. And when he arrives home, his wife and children do the same. His life, it seems, is owned by others. Everyone is sucking energy out of him, but they are not giving him the space to put energy back in.

David regards the gray suit he wears to work each day as an icon for his whole life. He, his friends, his colleagues, dress the same, live in similar houses, share similar interests, and hold similar beliefs. Nothing, it seems, stamps his life as being *his* life; it is interchangeable with a thousand others.

Even his skin seems gray to him. The face he sees each morning in the shaving mirror is strained. No longer do his eyes sparkle; they feel dull, the lids heavy.

Despite his enormous acclaim and success, and despite the Nobel Prize, [Hermann] Hesse in his mature years suffered from the tragic and painful state of being separated from his true self, to which doctors refer offhandedly as depression.

Alice Miller

About a third of my cases are suffering from no clinically definable neurosis, but from the senselessness and emptiness of their lives. This can be described as the general neurosis of our time.

Carl Jung

His shoulders are always hunched forward. He grinds his teeth in his sleep. Often his stomach feels bloated, but medical tests provide no explanation.

Less than a decade to retirement—that is the thought with which David steels himself so that he can continue to show the world the face of a fulfilled civil servant.

"Dilbert" © 1992 Scott Adams. Reprinted with permission of United Media. All rights reserved.

Boredom: Mary, 27, Lawyer

Mary still recalls her dad's proud face on her graduation day five years ago. Now she has a great job in a prominent law firm. Her boss is the firm's star rainmaker. She becomes centrally involved in most of the major projects that come his way. He has told her she is on a fast track to partnership. A glittering future in her chosen career beckons.

How annoying, then, that an unwelcome thought keeps popping into her mind: *This is boring, boring, boring.* It's absurd, she tells herself—how can she be bored when she is involved in many of the biggest deals in town? She berates herself: *Grow up and get real. Work is about earning a living. Count your blessings that you have the skills to become a high earner.* And she knuckles down again to the task at hand.

Alas, the nagging voice keeps returning. Over the past year it has become more insistent. Mary finds the thought of progressing along the red career carpet laid before her strangely disturbing.

Most of us are willing to put up with lives that consist largely in doing jobs that are a bore, earning the means to seek relief from the tedium by intervals of hectic and expensive leisure. These intervals are supposed to be the real thing, the real purpose served by the necessary evil of work.

Alan Watts

A Sense of a Life Unlived: Joshua, 39, Manager

Joshua was, it seems, born to manage. Since completing an MBA at Stanford, he has worked in increasingly demanding roles for four multinationals. Now he is with a computer company, heading the operation in one of its major regional markets. From here he could go anywhere in the management world.

Yet for all his success, Joshua is haunted by a sense of having achieved nothing significant. He senses that he could and should have turned his capabilities to far greater account by working in a different field of endeavor: one that remains elusively beyond his imagination to picture.

Looking back on his life, he feels as if he has been a piece of flotsam floating on a current. Not once, he tells himself, has he made a genuine decision of far-reaching import, where he has consciously weighed up various options and actively shaped his own life.

Sometimes the image comes into his mind of himself as a baby, lying bright-eyed in his cradle: a bundle of potentialities just waiting to be realized and, when realized, sure to bring joy and vitality to himself as well as enriching the world in which he lives. He senses that he has not become the person that baby was capable of becoming. Only a few, and not the most potent, of those possibilities have been converted into realities.

This is a disturbing image, and Joshua chooses not to dwell on it. The die is set, he has commitments, and anyway he doesn't know what else he would do even if he had the chance. He hunkers down grimly to grind through the remaining years of his career.

> But to snuff it not knowing who you are and what you are capable of, I can't think of anything sadder than that.
>
> Mo Anthoine
> (mountaineer)

IF THIS IS SUCCESS, WHO NEEDS FAILURE?

Maggie, Phil, Joanna, David, Mary, Joshua—all have succeeded, and are succeeding, in their careers.

And their prize? Angst in its manifold forms.

Bitter and bored. Empty and weary. Estranged and isolated. Insecure and entrapped. Sensing wasted talents and lost opportunities. If that's how you want to be, go find a career.

> The mass of men lead lives of quiet desperation. What is called resignation is confirmed desperation.
>
> *Henry David Thoreau*

Bliss

[Babbitt is] the man who never followed his bliss. You may have a success in life, but then just think of it—what kind of life was it? What good was it—you've never done the thing you wanted to do in all your life. I always tell my students, go where your body and soul want to go. When you have the feeling, then stay with it, and don't let anyone throw you off.

JOSEPH CAMPBELL

YOUR FIRST OPTION: BE A BABBITT

A family—Dad, Mom, twelve-year-old boy—is eating out one night at a restaurant.

"Drink your tomato juice," the father abruptly orders his son.

"I don't want to," comes the reply.

Dad, in a louder voice, repeats his command.

Mom intervenes. "Don't make him do what he doesn't want to do."

Dad is horrified. "He can't go through life doing what he wants to do," he lectures his wife sternly. "If he only does what he wants to do, he'll be dead.

Look at me. *I've never done a thing I wanted to in all my life.*"

This conversation in a restaurant in Bronxville, New York, is overheard. Sitting at the next table is Joseph Campbell, a young university teacher. When he hears the final remark, a thought instantly pops into his mind: *My God, there's Babbitt incarnate!*

Babbitt? Who's Babbitt?

You know him all right, you know him well. *Homo babbittus* is everywhere.

The archetype of the species is George F. Babbitt, hero of Sinclair Lewis's 1920 novel *Babbitt*. His chosen career is realty. Economically and socially, this career serves him well. He has to pay a heavy price, however: the subjugation of his individuality, the loss of his soul.

Babbitt's life is dedicated to the pursuit of social standing. He is desperate to be admitted, respected, liked, accepted. But he is plagued by angst. His inner self keeps pointing out the emptiness and falseness of his life. The more ruthlessly he pursues conformity, the more his anxieties plague him.

Babbitt wants so much to believe that the life he is living is the right one. Unfulfilling as it is, it still provides an illusion of security and meaning. Overturn it, and what would there be? Freedom is terrifying to one who, like Babbitt, lacks a solidly founded sense of self.

Over time, Babbitt finds himself unable any longer to shut out the inner voice telling him that the life he is living is false. For a few months he tries to escape from the straitjacket and rediscover his lost self. He commits small acts of rebellion: supporting a labor leader to the dismay of his friends, having an affair. But in the end he is unable to make a fresh start; he is just too typecast. He resigns himself to eking what satisfactions he can out of a real estate agent's life.

It is on the book's final page that Babbitt makes the

> Practically, I've never done a single thing I've wanted to in my whole life! I don't know's I've accomplished anything except just get along. I figure out I've made about a quarter of an inch out of a possible one hundred rods.
>
> *George Babbitt*

confession to his son that Joseph Campbell heard repeated in the restaurant: "I've never done a single thing I've wanted to in my whole life."

This is the price paid by Babbitt for ignoring his own inner truths and following a career that held no meaning for him.

YOUR SECOND OPTION: FOLLOW YOUR BLISS

Babbitt had a career. It brought him angst. A career will being *you* angst, too. If you want to avoid angst, you need, in Joseph Campbell's words, to "follow your bliss."

Following your bliss, says Campbell, means going "where your body and soul want to go." You need to seek out experiences that go beyond "food, shelter, progeny, and wealth." The key is to identify the things that stir you deep inside, the things that make you "not excited, not just thrilled, but deeply happy." Having discovered them, stick with them, found your life upon them, for therein lies your destiny.

Which is precisely what Joseph Campbell himself did. Entering adulthood, he dutifully joined the family business, where a safe and profitable career was assured. But sensing that he needed more out of life than the business could offer, he embarked on many years of study, writing, teaching, and travel. This was a time of exploration. He circled around, and gradually zeroed in on, his area of bliss. When he finally arrived there, he was nearly forty years old. And what was his bliss? Mythology. For the rest of his marvelously full life, he studied, taught, and wrote about mythology, and in time became the world's foremost authority on the subject.

> Revisit those moments of profound pleasure when every beating pulse echoed James Joyce's Irish heroine, Molly Bloom, in her flowing surrender to passion: *And yes I said yes I will Yes.*
>
> Sarah Ban Breathnach

Geese and the Meaning of Life

I remember the first time I played tennis on a real court. . . . The moment I stepped onto that crunchy red clay, felt the grit under my sneakers, felt the joy of smacking a ball over the net, I knew I was in the right place. I was probably about six years old when that happened, but I can remember it as if it was yesterday.

Martina Navratilova

Another who followed his bliss is Peter Scott, the English wildlife painter. From a young age, Scott was interested in natural history—which is perhaps not surprising since his father was the legendary Antarctic explorer Robert Falcon Scott. He studied zoology, but his true passion was sitting out in the marshlands in a punt, observing geese on the wing and painting them. Midcourse he changed tack and began to study art. As he later recalled, "My primary objective in life changed. Instead of a scientist I would be an artist. I have never regretted this great and momentous decision, for at one sweep my whole outlook on life was changed and enlarged. I saw it as the missing half which had suddenly come up into balance." Studying and painting wildlife, especially geese on the wing, became Scott's bliss, and the foundation of his life.

Painting geese on the wing? Would you choose to dedicate your life to this pursuit? How about the study of comparative mythology? I doubt it. And that's the point. Bliss is utterly personal. What stirs *you* deep inside bores *me* silly. What has profound meaning for me is as exciting as boiled cabbage to you.

The particular organism that is you has a deep and abiding passion. That is your bliss. It may be stars or cars. It may be mollusks or molecules. It may be bytes or rights. It may be minds or movies. It may be retailing or drain laying. It may be gods or gophers. It may be cosmetics or politics. Whatever it is, your bliss can't be explained, it can't be justified, it can't be rationalized— it just *is*.

Take Joseph Campbell, for example. His interest in mythology was not educated into him; it was part of his protoplasm. Myths connected at a primal level with

HOMER'S
CHICKEN
SANCTUARY

Suddenly, Homer knew what he was destined to paint.

something at the very heart of his being. They were, for him, a domain of ultimate meaning.

And Peter Scott? His pursuit—painting geese—was also intensely personal and spiritual, an activity of ultimate meaning. He summed up the essence of his life's work in just a few words: "The pursuit of beauty and truth are the two most exciting aspirations of the human spirit. So I am a painter by profession and an amateur scientist."

THE BAD NEWS IS, IT'S NOT AS EASY AS IT SOUNDS

"Follow your bliss"—it sounds so easy, but in truth it is far from that. Why is it so hard?

In the first place, it requires courage to leave the

Some people think football is a matter of life and death. I don't like that attitude. I can assure them it is much more serious than that.

*Bill Shankly
(soccer manager)*

broad paths of convention trodden by millions of other feet and to chart your own way through life. Obstacles bar the way: fear, self-doubt, disapproval. You need to overcome these obstacles if you are to live a life that has true meaning in terms of the idiosyncratic mysteries within you.

And here is an even bigger barrier: You need to *find* your bliss before you can follow it. From early on in life, you are bombarded with messages that teach you to distrust or shut out your own inner voice. By the time you are thirty, your parents, peers, schools, the media, and other social institutions may have so molded you that you no longer acknowledge your real self, the self that resides in your protoplasm. So you need to learn afresh to recognize your bliss.

> The world is full of people who have stopped listening to themselves or who have listened only to their neighbors to learn what they ought to do, how they ought to behave, and what the values are that they should be living for.
> *Joseph Campbell*

THE GOOD NEWS IS, MYTHS SERVE AS A GUIDEBOOK

If you want to know what to expect on your quest for bliss, you need only turn to Joseph Campbell's beloved myths. For it is with this quest that the basic myth is concerned. Mythic heroes leave the safety and protection of their home, community, or society and set off into the unknown on a hazardous adventure (in other words, to find their bliss). Along the way they face numerous trials and temptations that test their resolve (that is, their own fears, the opposition of others, and the seductive safety offered by convention). If they have the courage to persevere, they are assisted by supernatural forces (destiny). Eventually they discover treasure or become the possessor of magical powers (they find their bliss). They use such powers, upon their return home, to benefit or enrich their people.

Here, in a nutshell, is how Campbell translates the

story. You have to make a choice. Are you going to stick with the safe and familiar bounds of the known? Or will you follow your bliss, which involves venturing forth into the unknown to explore the mysteries of your inner being? It takes great courage to pursue the second course. If, however, you can muster that courage, your journey of self-discovery will revitalize you and equip you to unleash the full power of your natural gifts. This will have two powerful effects.

Finding Your Destiny

The first effect is that, by placing your life in tune with the forces of your own unique nature, you will achieve fulfillment and a deep sense of rightness, a sense that the life you are living is the life you ought to be living. Doors will open for you; opportunities will present themselves. You will discover your destiny.

Let's face it, in the hierarchy of sound career choices, the study of myths and the painting of geese do not rank high. Here is one speech Dad will never make: "Barbie, this idea of becoming a doctor is crazy. Drop it. Get into ancient fairy tales. And as for you, Ken, where did you get this dumb scheme of becoming a cost accountant? Become a geese painter instead." Yet Campbell and Scott, following their bliss, undertook these very pursuits. As a result, they enjoyed lives of astonishing richness (and, incidentally, reaped not insignificant material rewards).

Enriching the World

The second effect of following your bliss is that, by unlocking your own essence, you will fuel your vitality. This will equip you to vitalize the world around you. By unleashing your natural powers, you will benefit your community or society far more than if you had never ventured beyond the safe and conventional.

Again, look at Joseph Campbell and Peter Scott.

One day in July 1876, the young Henry Ford was riding with his father in a horse-drawn wagon towards Detroit, when he saw a steam engine coming towards him, propelled by its own power.

"I remember that engine," he declared forty-seven years later, "as though I had seen it only yesterday."

It was the first vehicle not drawn by horses that Henry Ford had ever seen. "I was off the wagon and talking to the engineer before my father, who was driving, knew what I was up to."

... Henry Ford always regarded his encounter with the moving engine as his meeting on the road to Damascus. He had come face to face with his destiny.

Robert Lacey
(Ford biographer)

Through their work, they sought to uncover meanings personal to them. But in so doing, they communicated a sense of truth and beauty that has enriched the lives of millions.

THE CHOICE YOU FACE

So there's the choice: Babbitt or bliss.

It's all too easy to choose Babbitt. If you do, you may achieve a healthy bank balance and public esteem. But that's all. Choose bliss, on the other hand, and you will develop an enduring, deep-seated sense of well-being and fulfillment.

Have you chosen a Babbitt-like career already? Then muster the courage to change course. You still have time aplenty to find and follow your bliss.

Once, after a game in Denver, my sister-in-law dropped by the locker room and told me that she'd broken into tears watching me coach. "I started crying," she said, "because I realized that this is exactly what you were meant to do. You're so comfortable out there. It just seems so right."

Phil Jackson

THREE

Callings and Careers

I compose because I am made for that and cannot do otherwise.

IGOR STRAVINSKY

YES, YOU TOO HAVE A CALLING

Picture Claude Monet lying in bed at six o'clock on a cold Monday morning, November 1908. A bell rings. He groans, buries his head under the pillow, reaches out one arm, and hurls the alarm clock against the wall. Ten minutes later, he drags his reluctant body out of bed.

"Another bloody day at the easel," he grumbles to his wife. "Water lilies, water lilies, more bloody water lilies. I never want to see another [expletive deleted] water lily in my life."

"Quit your moaning," replies Mme. Monet. "In another two months we'll have paid off the new living-room suite, and then we can start saving for that two-week vacation in Dijon."

Monet shuffles despondently off to the bathroom.

[Michael Jordan] was joyous about practices, joyous about games, as if he could not wait for either. Not many players had that kind of love.

David Halberstam

Doesn't quite ring true, does it? That's because painting wasn't Monet's job. It wasn't his career. It was his *calling*.

Okay, you might be thinking, *so Monet had a calling— what's that got to do with me? He was lucky, he was born with artistic talent, which gave him a calling. The world is divided into the lucky few who have a calling and the unlucky masses who don't. Monet was one of the lucky few, but I belong to the unlucky masses. I need to face up to that reality.*

Wrong. You have a calling, too. You just haven't discovered it yet. Or maybe you *have* discovered it but haven't recognized it for what it is. Or perhaps you've recognized it but haven't been able to muster the courage to follow it.

Everyone has a calling. That includes you. It's out there waiting for you.

WHAT IS A CALLING?

Now I am able to say—it is an antique word, and it is one that is easily scoffed at—but I do have a sense of vocation. And I have it, I will have it to the last ounce of my life, the last second. I have this sense, and I'm proud that I've got it, and I am no longer ashamed of saying this, I have, and have had, a sense of vocation. And it was writing.

Dennis Potter
(television playwright, in an interview two weeks before his death from cancer)

These days the word *calling* has a rather quaint ring. As with its synonym *vocation*, its popular usage is largely confined to religious, artistic, or extremely public-spirited types. You would have no trouble talking of a missionary, a weaver, a doctor who works with underprivileged children in the Third World, as pursuing their calling. But you would think it bizarre to describe a stockbroker, an undertaker, a mechanic, as pursuing their calling. They, you would say, have a career, not a calling.

This distinction is nonsense. A calling is simply something you are called to do. Called by whom or what? Called by you yourself, from deep within. Your bliss is your calling.

No type of work is, by its very nature, a calling. And no type of work is, by its very nature, incapable of being a calling.

Dominic, for example, is passionate about his work. It is his calling. And what is it? Pest eradication! Now, catching rats may not be your idea of bliss, but it is undoubtedly Dominic's. Rats fascinate him, as do mice, possums, cockroaches, ants, even pesky seagulls. He once managed a large eradication business, but managing took him away from fieldwork, his first love. So he formed his own two-person firm, which specializes in taking on difficult jobs that have defeated bigger companies with their standardized solutions. These jobs give him the chance to (as he puts it) "get inside the mind" of the pest and devise a unique eradication strategy.

Ask Dominic why he loves his work so much, and he will reply, "I'm always learning." Given half a chance, he will enlighten you with his latest astonishing discoveries about the habits and habitats, sex lives and diets of the stoat, the blowfly, or the carpet beetle. As you hear him describe how he pits his wits against their instincts, you may find yourself believing with him that pest eradication is the most creative pursuit known to humanity.

The fundamental difference, then, between a calling and a career lies not in the intrinsic nature of the work, but in the motivation with which it is undertaken. A calling is, first and foremost, something you do to express a passion flowing from your innermost being. A career is, first and foremost, something you do to derive external rewards—material possessions, financial security, social status, or the approval of others.

OF NUNS AND LAWYERS

Peggy and Geraldine are nuns. Their lives, devoted to service and prayer, are on the surface more or less identical. Peggy's decision to become a nun was one she made for herself. Never for a moment has she regretted

My devotion to the ANC and the struggle was unremitting. This disturbed Evelyn [Nelson Mandela's first wife]. She had always assumed that politics was a youthful diversion, that I would some day return to the Transkei and practice there as a lawyer. . . . We had many arguments about this, and I patiently explained to her that politics was not a distraction but my lifework, that it was an essential and fundamental part of my being.

Nelson Mandela

> When I was writing I was expressing my own higher Self.... Two paragraphs into the writing of my first book, when I was twenty-three years old, I knew I had come home, found myself, found my purpose, found my god. I have since never doubted it once.
>
> *Ken Wilber*

it. Friends in the outside world have sometimes commended her on her life of self-sacrifice. Her reply has been quick and firm: "No, it is not a question of self-sacrifice. I am not doing this out of an altruistic desire to serve others. I am doing it because serving God brings me joy." Geraldine, on the other hand, became a nun to satisfy a moral code drummed into her from birth. She performs, dutifully, as many good deeds as Peggy, but a sense of emptiness secretly afflicts her. This she cannot understand. She wonders why she doesn't radiate contentment like Peggy. The reason is plain: For Peggy, being a nun is a calling; for Geraldine, it is not.

Terry and Marcus are partners in a commercial law firm. The law is Terry's passion. He reveres it, regards it indeed as almost sacred, the crowning glory of humankind's achievements. Marcus, in contrast, is a lawyer because it seemed to him fifteen years ago, and still seems, the best way open to him to earn a good income and achieve some social standing. He is as successful a lawyer as Terry, but nowhere near as fulfilled. He dreams of winning the lottery and quitting the law—though ask him what he would do instead, and he has no idea. Terry is in his bliss; Marcus is ruled by angst. For Terry, the practice of law is a calling; for Marcus, it is a career.

CALLING VERSUS CAREER

- *Bliss versus angst:* A calling brings you bliss. A career brings you angst.
- *Internally driven versus externally driven:* A calling is a response to a call from deep within. A career is driven by a desire for external satisfactions such as money, approval, or status.
- *Holistic versus fragmented:* A calling engages your whole person, body and soul. Your person-

ality, your values, your passions, your skills—all are deployed in the service of that which has most meaning in your life.

A career picks and chooses which parts of you it wants. It exploits those parts that have value in terms of the job to be done. It is not interested in—may in fact disdain, even trample on—other parts. It may, for example, value your analytical skills, but regard as irrelevant your nurturing skills. It may value your honesty in dealing with your boss, but encourage you to trade in half-truths in dealing with the world outside on his or her behalf. It may value your ability to juggle several difficult projects at once, but be utterly unsympathetic toward your stress. It may value the skills you bring to the task, but dismiss the boredom you suffer. It may value your being a conscientious employee, but stop you from being a conscientious parent.

A career, in short, takes fragments and separates them out from the rest of your being. *Bring the fragments into work,* it says, *but leave the rest of you at home.*

- *Integrated versus compartmentalized:* In a calling, your work is an expression of your essential self, and therefore an integrated part of your life. Monet was not working when he painted water lilies; he was simply being Monet. In fact, he was never more truly Monet than when he was standing in front of a canvas with brush in hand. Similarly for Rudolf Nureyev: His dancing was, in the words of one biographer, "both the means of his living and the end. It is not a gesture for the benefit of others but an instinctive egoistic existential act. He can say, paraphrasing Descartes, 'Je danse donc je suis'—'I dance therefore I am.'"

You may sometimes talk of being "absorbed"

> I had become very good at certain aspects of my work, but at the cost of distorting my personality. My family, my own sense of wholeness, had paid the price.... Words of praise and appreciation drowned out the still, small voice inside me which told me that I was leaving something out.
>
> *Harold Kushner*

> I do not believe that Gandhi needed to read any—let alone all—of these texts to arrive at his principles and principal modes of operation. Over the decades they sprang organically from his being.
>
> *Howard Gardner*

in a task. At such times, your ego, your conscious sense of being a separate person, seems to evaporate and you become utterly caught up in the activity of the moment. Often you are astonished to find that several hours have passed. And a feeling of inner peace possesses you. The word *absorbed* perfectly captures this idea, central to a calling, of the person and the work losing their separate identities and becoming integrated in a single process of being and doing.

A career, in contrast, makes work a distinct compartment of your life. You, the person, are here; the work activities to be accomplished, using mere fragments of your being, are out there, separate from you.

- *Growing versus shriveling:* Following your calling takes you inevitably on a journey of self-discovery. And with each new moment of discovery, you nurture those parts of you that are most fundamental to your being.

A career, with its fragmenting and compartmentalized focus, brings growth as well, but often a horrible, contorted growth. It develops only those parts of you that are functionally material in terms of the job to be done. It leaves other parts of you—parts that represent, potentially, the source of your bliss—to wither on the vine.

The result? Well, you end up a bit like a bodybuilder who has spent a decade developing only his right arm. Yes, you may have superb skills in job-related fragments. You may have a wonderful bank balance and a great reputation in your field. You may present to the world the persona of a confident achiever. But inside, at the core, you have shriveled. Little wonder that, for all your apparent success, you feel one-dimensional, empty, and insecure.

- *Renewing versus recycling:* With self-discovery comes renewal. A calling leads you ever onward. You are a different person tomorrow from today. You constantly take what you have discovered about yourself and apply it in new domains, in the process making further self-discoveries. It's a virtuous cycle.

  In a career, you recycle your skills and knowledge. Instead of getting five years' experience in a job, you may get one year's experience five times over. Sure, promotions and job changes provide some new experiences, but only in one compartment of your life. The "other" you, the one who does not come to work, is left to atrophy.

- *Engaged versus busy:* If you are in your calling, a heavy workload vitalizes you. Each task engages the core you, gives you another chance for self-discovery and self-expression.

  If you're in a career, a heavy workload oppresses you. Much of the time you're under pressure. You feel that the remorseless flow of work stops you from doing anything as well as you would like. You crave more time and space. Far from engaging you, each task is seen as just another thing to process in order that you can get on with the next task, then the next, and the next.

> Each added work brings with it an element of self-discovery. I must create in order to know myself, and since self-knowledge is a never-ending search, each new work is only a part-answer to the question "Who am I?" and brings with it the need to go on to other and different part-answers.
>
> *Aaron Copeland*
> *(composer)*

From "The Full Alex" published by Headline. Reprinted with permission of Peattie & Taylor.

- *Energized versus enervated:* Following your calling means living a life that is in tune with your nature. Because of this alignment, your natural energies flow as they are meant to. Work is a source of energy.

  When your work and your essential being are poorly aligned, you burn a huge amount of emotional energy coping with your angst. Not surprisingly, you often feel weary and flat at the end of a working day, as if a wringer has squeezed out all your energies. You may look forward to recharging your batteries on vacation, but all too often sickness strikes on your first day off, leaving you more enervated than ever.

- *Vital versus stale:* How do you feel if you're deploying your whole being, growing, renewing yourself constantly, absorbed in what you're doing and energized by it? In a word, *alive.* Such vitality is way out of your reach if you are imprisoned in a career. Denied the chance to be yourself, you feel, at best, half alive.

- *Life-affirming versus life-denying:* To follow your calling means to say yes to the marvelous, mysterious endowments of nature that reside at the very heart of your being. It means to celebrate those unique endowments by developing and using them as nature intended. It means to be, in Søren Kierkegaard's words, "the self that you truly are."

  If, on the other hand, you lock yourself in a career, you deny the things that make you unique, the things that are potentially the noblest aspects of your being. You don a corset to make yourself fit a conventional form, even though that means contorting what nature has given you. Instead of living your own life, you

Some people marvel at the energy I put into my work. What they don't understand is that this is not a job in the sense of having to go to work. It's a great experience.

Irving Shapiro
(CEO of DuPont)

live a life defined by others. As the years roll on, you ponder regretfully on might-have-beens. You cannot escape a sense of life possibilities unrealized.

- *Difficult versus easy:* It is difficult to find and follow your calling. Recall the hero's quest described in the last chapter. You have to leave behind the safe and familiar world of convention and make your own way, overcoming your own fears and self-doubts as well as the disapproval of others. It can be a long and arduous journey.

In contrast, a career is easy. Here is an infallible Five-Step Plan:

Step 1: Work out what you're good at.

Step 2: Take no account of what for you is enjoyable and meaningful.

Step 3. Out of the things you're good at, select one that will bring solid financial and social rewards.

Step 4: Keep at it, stoically. Remorselessly move onward and upward.

Step 5: Whenever a little voice inside you has the gall to ask, *Is this* really *what I want to spend my allotted time on this planet doing?*—ignore it at all costs.

Ironically, many who contemplate leaving their careers tell themselves, or are told by others, that to do so would amount to "wimping out." Wrong! The opposite is true. Staying where you are, not being true to yourself, not fighting the forces of inertia, not challenging your fears—*that* is the easy course. That is the option for wimps.

You hear that bird outside the window? He's a mockingbird. He don't have a sound of his own. He copies everybody's sound, and you don't want to do that. You want to be your own man, have your own sound. That's what it's really about. So, don't be nobody else but yourself. You know what you got to do and I trust your judgment.

Advice given to jazz
musician Miles Davis
by his father

On this narrow planet, we have only the choice between two unknown worlds. One of them tempts us—ah! what a dream, to live in that!—the other stifles us at the first breath.

Colette

CALLING VERSUS CAREER	
CALLING	CAREER
Bliss	Angst
Internally driven	Externally driven
Holistic	Fragmented
Integrated	Compartmentalized
Growing	Shriveling
Renewing	Recycling
Engaged	Busy
Energized	Enervated
Vital	Stale
Life-affirming	Life-denying
Difficult	Easy

BUT I'M NOT ENTITLED TO HAVE A CALLING

Jessie is a young doctor. She is good at her work, but for her it is definitely a career and not a calling. When she talks about work alternatives, two truly excite her. But she seems to grasp for reasons not to pursue them. What is it that holds her back?

A major barrier for Jessie is a set of attitudes about what she is entitled to expect from life, and in particular from work. "A job," she says, "is basically about earning a living and gaining some social respectability. It's naive to hope for more than that. All this talk about pursuing something that would bring me joy is self-indulgent. It makes me feel guilty."

This idea that work is by its nature a necessary evil to be endured pervades our society. It is underpinned by two assumptions. First, *If it hurts, it must be good for me.* Second, *If it's fun, then it's self-centered and irresponsible.*

If people believe that they are not entitled to find enjoyment and meaning in their work, it is understand-

> Sometimes it seems as if we live out our lives in the attic of the house of our being, rarely visiting the first and second floors and never the basement, which is locked.
>
> *Jean Houston*

able that they choose suffocating careers. Not only do they choose such careers but they remain in them, offering at most passive resistance, even while the suffocation continues.

Ron, a depressed forty-six-year-old hospital administrator, puts it this way. "I grizzle about work, but that's not really fair. The fact is, I expect too much from work. Instead of expecting to enjoy work, I should make better use of my spare time. I don't have any hobbies, I don't nurture friendships."

Ron is right to this extent: He does need to start making better use of his spare time. But he is more wrong than right. His work consumes the bulk of his waking hours and his energies from Monday to Friday, and often in the weekend as well. How can he possibly expect to lead a rich and fulfilling life if he uses only his residual hours and energies for that purpose?

This is precisely the point his colleague Carl makes to him. Carl is frustrated by Ron's passivity because it mirrors his own of a few years back. Carl, you see, has "been there and done that." Six years ago, he was much as Ron is today: a middle manager who accepted boredom as an inevitable ingredient of work. But then fate intervened: The insurance company that employed him merged with another and Carl was laid off. This crisis forced him into a prolonged and sometimes painful period of self-examination. He moved out of financial services and into health care, a field much more closely aligned to his values. Now he looks back on his downsizing as a marvelous blessing that jolted him from merely subsisting to truly living.

> For all of us, the key is to pay close attention to which activities make us feel most alive and in love with life—and then try to spend as much time as possible engaged in those activities.
> *Nathaniel Branden*

YOUR RIGHT AND DUTY

If Jessie and Ron are ever to regain a sense of inner well-being, it is imperative that, like Carl, they challenge their

I, as I now know myself, am not the final form of my being. We must constantly die one way or another to the selfhood already achieved.

Joseph Campbell

entrenched attitudes to work, and realign their working lives in the direction of their bliss.

Do you need to as well? You do unless you believe that, like Monet, you have a calling.

Not only are you entitled to pursue this calling, you have a duty to do so. And it is this duty, with its biological source, that we turn to consider in the next chapter.

The Elements

FOUR

Your Core Self

To thine own self be true.

SHAKESPEARE (*HAMLET*)

DNA

In the beginning was your Core Self.

It burst into being, encoded in your DNA molecules, at the moment of your conception. It contained everything that you were capable of becoming: physical potentialities like height, hair color, and the shape of your little toe, but also potentialities of the mind, the emotions, the spirit.

Your Core Self predates your birth. It predates your upbringing. It predates your schooling. It predates your adolescence. It predates your meeting those who have loved you, those who have mentored you, those who have hurt you. It predates your various jobs. It predates your friendships. It predates your family responsibilities. It predates your work obligations. It predates your life.

[As a young girl] I was suddenly and overwhelmingly struck with the greatest revelation of all: that I was an individual person different from anyone of the world. It happened quite unaccountably in mid-afternoon, and I stood stock-still for several minutes, just where I was at the foot of the stairs, pondering on this strange new idea.

Margot Fonteyn

33

Had you been plucked from your cradle at birth and dropped down in another continent with another culture, and been brought up by other parents, and gone to other schools, and had other lovers and other jobs, you would still have had the same Core Self.

Your Core Self contains your essence, the absolute, intrinsic nature of your being, the primal, pulsating life force within you. Treasure it, revere it, because therein lies the source of your bliss. Therein lies the calling that's waiting for you.

YOU'RE UNIQUE, YOU'RE A FREAK

Our birth is but a sleep and a forgetting;
The Soul that rises with us, our life's Star,
Hath had elsewhere its setting
And cometh from afar.

William Wordsworth

Think about it: the direct lineage of your Core Self. Go back beyond your parents, and your parents' parents. Go back a hundred years, a thousand years, a hundred thousand—you're now at the dawn of *Homo sapiens*. Keep going back—a million years, ten million years, a hundred million, five hundred million, one billion years. Then double all that to two billion years. And double it yet again, to four billion years. It was nearly that long ago that the first single-celled creatures—your ancestors—came into being in the primeval soup.

Yes, you're the unique product of billions of years of evolution. Organism upon organism, of which only a tiny fraction have been hominid, have procreated over the ages to produce you. No other being, living now or in the past, has the same Core Self as you.

Not only are you unique, but you're a freak. You shouldn't be here. If just one creature in that extraordinary chain of innumerable lives had succumbed to predation, disease, starvation, thirst, flood, fire, or accident before the act of procreation that perpetuated the lineage, the unique being that sprang into life at the instant of your conception wouldn't be here.

Your ancestors lived charmed lives indeed. They

managed to survive the mass extinctions that on five occasions devastated life on earth: the Ordovician 430 million years ago, the Devonian 350 million years ago, the Permian 225 million years ago, the Triassic 200 million years ago, and the Cretaceous 65 million years ago. Each of these wiped out most species then living, but your ancestors were made of hardy (or lucky) stock, and they survived.

Your Core Self is truly an astonishing, odds-defying miracle. Don't you think you owe it some respect?

> Men go forth to wonder at the heights of mountains, the huge waves of the sea, the vast compass of the ocean, the courses of the stars; and they pass by themselves without wondering.
>
> *St. Augustine*

THE DUTY YOU OWE TO NATURE

Søren Kierkegaard wrote 150 years ago that the goal of life is "to be that self which one truly is." Which self are you going to be? That which flows out of your Core Self? Or a different, and false, self?

You are like any other organism in this respect: Your Core Self pulsates with a life force that drives it to grow, to realize its innate possibilities. Nature has given you faculties for a purpose: They are there to be used. You owe a duty to nature to use them.

To honor the life force within you and be true to your Core Self, follow your bliss. Because it is by following your bliss, through your calling, that you grow the most sublime of your potentialities.

Alternatively, you can do what most people do: Deny your Core Self, lock it away, and base your life on a different self, one that is constructed not out of your own essential nature but out of what other people consider right.

> The aim of the life of a rosebud is to be all that is inherent as potentiality in the rosebush: that its leaves are well developed and that its flower is the most perfect rose that can grow out of this seed.
>
> *Erich Fromm*

INGRID'S PLIGHT

Ingrid was a polar bear. Born in captivity, she spent most of her life in a zoo. She lived in a concrete enclosure, painted white. For exercise she could dive into a thirty-yard-long pool, or she could pace along a flat platform beside the pool.

In this environment Ingrid had no chance of becoming the creature she was meant to be. Her inner being yearned for the vast open spaces of the Arctic. That primal yearning having been thwarted, she became neurotic. Her ceaseless pacing from side to side within her enclosure reflected not only an imprisoned body but an imprisoned spirit as well. Her death mercifully liberated her from an utterly false life.

What happened to Ingrid shows what will happen to you if your Core Self is denied, if your innate drive to grow toward your potentialities is shackled. Just like Ingrid, you have a need to be what you truly are. And what you truly are derives from the unique biological endowment contained in your Core Self. Be true to your Core Self and you will find bliss. Violate your Core Self and you condemn yourself to angst.

How the Core Self Is Subjugated

The trouble is, it is tough to stay in touch with your Core Self. It becomes encrusted with the detritus of life. Starting from your earliest days out of the womb, you learn to distrust your own experience of truth. You learn to deny your own feelings and perceptions. You learn the games people play. You learn society's rules and conventions, and you come to define yourself in terms of social roles.

You are a son or daughter. You're also a wife or husband. You're a sister or brother or cousin or uncle or aunt. You're a friend. You're a member. You're a fan. You're a colleague. You're a manager or a worker. You're a clerk, or an architect, or a firefighter, or a nurse, or a preacher. You're unemployed. You're a

---

Jesus said, "If you bring forth what is within you, what you bring forth will save you. If you do not bring forth what is within you, what you do not bring forth will destroy you."

The Gospel of Thomas

Obviously *Karaoke* [a television play] is a metaphor.... There's the music and you have your little line and you can sing it and everything is written for you. That is the way life appears . . . and feels to a lot of people.

Dennis Potter

homeowner, you're a tenant. You're a debtor, you're a creditor. You're a consumer. You're a taxpayer. You're a citizen. You're a . . . but hold it! Where's the Core Self gone? By now it's so encrusted, you don't even know it's there, let alone what it wants you to be.

It is, of course, only natural that you should play numerous social roles. You're a human being—which is to say, you're a social creature. In evolutionary terms, you belong to a society because societies improve the survival prospects of *Homo sapiens*.

Some conflict between your social roles and your individual drives is inevitable. Carl Jung wrote of this conflict at length. Social roles, he said, necessarily constrain "the innate idiosyncrasy of a living being." Any social goal can be attained "only at the cost of a diminution of personality."

As with so many things in life, it is all a question of balance. Socialization is essential. The problem occurs when it is carried too far, resulting in subjugation of fundamental aspects of your Core Self.

In the modern world of powerful governments, giant bureaucracies, and huge corporations, such subjugation is increasingly common. It suits all of them if people toe the line, accept the system. How can an individual be expected to stand up to such enormous pressures?

This is the issue with which Mahatma Gandhi was preoccupied throughout his long life, says his biographer Louis Fischer. "How can the modern individual maintain his inner peace and outer security, how can he remain honest, free, and himself in the face of the assaults being made upon him by the power of mighty governments, the power of mighty economic organizations, the power of evil that resides in cruel majorities and militant minorities, and the power now extractable from the atom?" Gandhi understood why most people felt unable to do other than submit to these agglomerations of power, but was alarmed at the consequence: "a shrinking man."

> This is the threat to our lives that we all face today. Is the system going to flatten you out and deny you your humanity, or are you going to be able to make use of the system to the attainment of human purposes?
>
> *Joseph Campbell*

The system, of course, provides the illusion of catering to your individual tastes, especially through the abundance of consumer goods it churns out. You can choose for your standardized world from a bewildering array of cars, PDAs, lamp shades, ties, knick-knacks, and noodles. Or you can be one of those who introduce a bit of color into their standard uniform, thus allowing themselves, as Ernest Becker put it, "to stick out, but ever so little and so safely, with a red ribbon or a red boutonnière, but not with head and shoulders." Your world remains, at core, a standardized world.

Your parents, teachers, and employers, themselves the product of the same system, add to the pressures on you to conform. Understandably, they strive to equip you with the skills needed to fit into the system. Education has become largely about preparing you for a good job. What is often lost sight of is the essence of education. "Surely," wrote Indian philosopher Krishnamurti, "education has no meaning unless it helps you to understand the vast expanse of life with all its subtleties, with its extraordinary beauty, its sorrows and joys. You may win degrees . . . and land a very good job; but then what? What is the point of it all if in the process your mind becomes dull, weary, stupid? . . . Not to imitate but to discover—*that* is education, is it not?"

Not only do the social roles of modern life fail to respect your uniqueness. They also, all too often, fail to

> It is very easy to conform to what your society or your parents and teachers tell you. That is a safe and easy way of existing; but that is not living, because in it there is fear, decay, death. To live is to find out for yourself what is true.
>
> *Krishnamurti*

meet your basic social needs. How many city dwellers feel desperately lonely and isolated even though millions of others live within a few miles of their doorstep?

The environment in which you live is a far cry from your ancestral environment, the one that fits your genetic makeup. Your genes equip you to live in a stable, low-tech community of extended families whose members seldom travel more than a few miles from their birthplace. Instead you find yourself inserted into a world of nuclear families living among shifting suburban populations, cars and jet airplanes, canned laughter and drive-in weddings, electric toothbrushes and mobile telephones, artificial grass and polluted air. On an evolutionary time scale, this radical change in environment has occurred in the twinkling of an eye—far too fast to permit any genetic adaptation.

All in all, it is little wonder if you have become estranged from your Core Self. From early childhood your life has been channeled toward conventional social roles. By middle age, you may have become a mere cipher, living the life that society wants you to live, conforming to the expectations of others, materially gluttonous while starving emotionally and spiritually.

THE CORE SELF RECLAIMED

If pursuing social goals has caused you to lose sight of your Core Self, all is not lost. It is still there. Deep in your being, there remain what Carl Jung called "glowing coals among gray ashes." It is not too late; these coals can still be fanned into life.

Here is how the violinist Nigel Kennedy reclaimed his individuality. Early on in his career, well before he had achieved fame and fortune as a concert violinist, a chance came his way that any talented young violinist would kill for: to play Elgar's Violin Concerto at London's Festival Hall, under the baton of Yehudi Menuhin.

> When one is a stranger to oneself, then one is estranged from others too.
>
> *Anne Morrow Lindbergh*

> I hope that if anything of what I am trying to do is attractive to youngsters, then it will be my independence: that what I've been able to do shows you can nurture your own expressions. Whatever talents you have locked away inside—they are very precious and 100 percent you.
>
> *Nigel Kennedy*

He dedicated himself to pleasing the maestro, who held strong views on how the piece should be played. He wanted his audience to think, "This young man plays just like Menuhin"—what higher praise could there be? And he succeeded. The critics said Kennedy's performance was very similar to Menuhin's. But puzzlingly, they didn't seem to regard this as a virtue.

While Kennedy was reflecting on all this, the penny dropped. It wasn't good enough for him to imitate someone else, even someone as revered as Menuhin. His task was to reveal himself—his *true* self—to his audience. In his own words: "It was time to tear down all those indoctrinated values . . . I had to face a really massive reclamation process to reestablish my own individuality . . . I now had to start asserting myself."

Kennedy realized that he had to stop his slavish imitation of his teachers. Learning their rules and conventions was fine, as long as he then deployed them in expressing his own Core Self, with which he had lost touch during his period of immersion in the techniques of the masters. The starting point was to get closer to his own core self, with which he had lost touch during his period of immersion in the techniques of the masters. In his own apt phrase, he had to "journey back toward individuality."

> In the coming world, they will not ask me, "Why were you not Moses?" They will ask me, "Why were you not Zusya?"
>
> *Rabbi Zusya*

YOUR CORE SELF'S THREE NEEDS

Your Core Self yearns to be allowed to express itself. This desire has three distinct but interrelated dimensions:

- Skill: Your Core Self wants you to engage in activities that use your innate abilities.
- Enjoyment: Your Core Self wants you to engage in activities that you find intrinsically enjoyable.
- Meaning: Your Core Self wants you to engage in activities that for you have meaning.

Celebrated Canadian stress researcher Hans Selye puts it this way. You should select an environment that is "in line with your innate preferences—find an activity which you like and respect." He continues: "The art is to find, among the jobs you are capable of doing, the one you really like best." It's all there, in those two sentences. You should engage in activities that match "the innate preferences" that are unique to your Core Self. They should be activities that you are "capable of doing" (skill), that you "like" doing (enjoyment), and that you "respect" (meaning).

Let's now consider each of these three dimensions in turn.

> Life must be allowed to run its natural course toward the fulfillment of its innate potential. To a biologist, this represents a pretty fair equivalent of what men of God, sages and philosophers would call the aim of life.
>
> *Hans Selye*

FIVE

Skill

*Prisoner, God has given you good abilities, instead of
which you go about the country stealing ducks.*

WILLIAM ARABIN

THE SKILLS MANTRA

"Don't drop out. Educate yourself. Become qualified.
Get skills."

This mantra is repeated endlessly to young people today.
But it begs a fundamental question, which is simply:
Why?

There are two reasons to get skills.* One is the right
reason; the other is the wrong reason. The reason
wouldn't matter if the result were the same. But it's not.
The right reason will cause you to get one set of skills;
the wrong reason will cause you to get a different set of
skills. And it is the first set that will better equip you for
your calling.

*Throughout this book, the word *skill* should be understood to
include any ability, competency, or knowledge.

THE RIGHT REASON

Why get skills? The right answer is simple: so that you can pursue your calling.

Your calling, whatever it is, will not be based on just any old skills. It will utilize your talents. These, as we shall see in chapter 22, are special abilities sourced in your Core Self. Your calling will, moreover, be challenging; it will tax you to grow your talents, to make as much of them as possible.

So which skills should you seek to develop? Your talents, of course, plus ancillary skills: the skills needed to explore, identify your talents, and follow your calling.

How should you develop them? Probably (but not necessarily—it depends on where your bliss happens to be found), you will need higher education. But higher education is not enough.

> The first and most important choice a leader makes is the choice to serve, without which one's capacity to lead is profoundly limited. That choice is not an action in the normal sense—it's not something you do, but an expression of your being.
>
> *Peter Senge*

Take, for example, the skills of a manager. Charles Handy writes of skills that no business school can teach: "perspicacity, ambition and tenacity, the ability to be tough and tender, to be able to work with people and to handle power but with responsibility, to have, even, some charm and a sense of humor." Are these skills peripheral to the core skills needed by managers? On the contrary, they *are* the core skills, and those taught by business schools are peripheral. That is why Handy advised those interviewing applicants for a management course to "look out, initially, for those who, in one sense, did not need to come."

The fact is that many of the critical skills you will require to pursue your calling are best developed through life experience. All too often this truth is forgotten or ignored. The result? Many young adults move directly from high school to college to graduate school to a career, missing out on the life experience that is needed to develop self-knowledge and essential life skills.

THE WRONG REASON

It is a cliché, but nevertheless true, that in the postindustrial age—or what is sometimes called the "information age"—the source of wealth and power is no longer property but knowledge. Cerebral skills—those to do with building, accessing, and deploying knowledge—are the world's most valuable assets.

Here, then, is an obvious reason to acquire skills: to equip yourself to earn a very good living. Medical, business, and law schools are full of students who are there for that very reason.

The trouble is, it's the wrong reason. Ask Maggie, Phil, Joanna, David, Mary, and Joshua, whom we met in chapter 1. All of them are skilled at what they do. All of them earn a good living. And all of them suffer from angst.

The simple fact is that being skilled at something may help you become rich, but by itself it won't help you discover your bliss. For that you need also to satisfy those two other dimensions of your Core Self's yearning to express itself: enjoyment and meaning.

> The moral flabbiness born of the exclusive worship of the bitch-goddess success. That—with the squalid cash interpretation put on the word success—is our national disease.
>
> *William James*

THE SPECIALIST'S TRAP

Basing your working life on things you are skilled at does not necessarily lead you *toward* happiness. It can

indeed lead you *away from* happiness. Especially if your skill is in a left-brained faculty—analysis, logic, rationality—its constant use can make you ever narrower. The world is full of highly skilled technical experts who are extremely clever at what they do but who lack the rounded knowledge and experience that is necessary for judgment and wisdom.

One of the saddest phenomena in the professions these days is the doctor who doesn't know how to listen. Unable to establish a proper person-to-person relationship with the patient, the doctor focuses on the symptoms and seeks to solve the problem entirely in technical terms. Not only is this bad news for the patient, but it is fundamentally unsatisfying for the doctor as well. Alas, this phenomenon is not confined to doctors. The old-style family lawyer who knew the client as a person and who gave wise counsel, not merely technical help, is becoming rare, too.

The narrowing of human values that a focus on skills can cause is evident too in the excesses of the financial services industry over the last two decades. Many banking and brokerage firms came to be dominated by young financial whiz kids. No doubt about it, they were highly skilled. Through the design of intricate structures and complex money-go-rounds, they achieved all manner of financial sleights of hand. However, being expert as technicians but unrounded as humans, they lacked an ethical base, which is why their machinations were often amoral, if not downright immoral.

THE SHIPWRECKED MARINER

In summary, acquiring skills is good, so long as your choice of skills is governed by the right factors. If you acquire skills in order to secure for yourself a good living, you will probably achieve a good living, but you

> I think, on the whole, we doctors are a very depressed group of people.... Practicing medicine is not much fun if you only write prescriptions and don't have the time to get to know your patients.
>
> *Dean Ornish*

> The trouble with the rat race is that even if you win you're still a rat.
>
> *Jane Wagner and Lily Tomlin*

will also achieve angst. If, on the other hand, you see your acquisition of skills as simply an aspect of the process of exploring and discovering your calling, letting earning a living be a by-product rather than a driving purpose, you will acquire a different set of skills. They will be skills that will eventually enable you to live a joyful and meaningful life.

Within the managerial and professional world there are many people who are both highly skilled and fulfilled. They are following their bliss. But they are greatly outnumbered by equally skilled but miserable colleagues.

When I look at them, an image of a shipwrecked mariner often pops into my mind. He is washed up on a desert island with three large crates. Feverishly he opens one, and finds that it is full of canned spinach and SPAM. For days, weeks, months, he keeps himself alive with these cans. He ignores the other two crates, for he can tell they do not contain food. But if he did open them, he would find the means of his salvation: for example, a fishing rod, an inflatable life raft, emergency beacons and a radio-telephone, tools, some of his favorite books, even a Discman and some much-loved CDs. So his desolate existence continues, consisting of numbing boredom interspersed with meals of spinach and SPAM.

The moral of this story? Just this. The crate the mariner opens represents skill. Sure, it puts food in his stomach. But by itself that is all it does. And the other two crates, unopened and ignored? They represent enjoyment and meaning, which feed heart and soul.

Rely on skill alone, and you will merely endure. Conjoin skill with enjoyment and meaning, and you will truly live.

There is an Indian proverb or axiom that says that everyone is a house with four rooms, a physical, a mental, an emotional, and a spiritual. Most of us tend to live in one room most of the time but, unless we go into every room every day, even if only to keep it aired, we are not a complete person.

Rumer Godden

Enjoyment

*People must not do things for fun. We are not here for fun.
There is no reference to fun in any Act of Parliament.*

A. P. HERBERT

THE SEGREGATION OF WORK AND LEISURE

In old Tom's eyes, they were cheats.

Bobby Jones. Ben Hogan. Sam Snead. Walter Hagen. Arnold Palmer. Jack Nicklaus. Great golfers all of them. But cheats. Not because they violated the rules of golf. Their transgression was far more serious than that. They violated the rules of life.

How? By getting paid for doing something they enjoyed. That was their foul deed.

You see, old Tom loved golf. But he was a child of the Great Depression. Those terrible years had instilled in him a deep-seated work philosophy. "If you have a job, count your blessings. Your job will enable you to

> The main thing is, every morning when I wake up, I go do something I really enjoy. How many people in the world can say that?
>
> *Tiger Woods*

pay the rent and put food on the table. Ask from it no more than that. Certainly don't expect to enjoy it."

Over time, old Tom's philosophy hardened. "Don't expect to enjoy your work" became "Expect not to enjoy your work." And he was not alone. Society joined him in segregating work and leisure. They were seen as opposites: work a matter of duty and necessity, leisure a matter of choice and enjoyment. They were mutually exclusive. By definition, leisure and its companion, enjoyment, were to be pursued only outside work hours.

"Doonesbury" © 1973. G. B. Trudeau. Reprinted with permission of Universal Press Syndicate. All rights reserved.

Sadly, the philosophy that work is not meant to be fun—indeed, that it is the antithesis of fun—continues to thrive today. Which is why you will see more happy faces in five minutes in any village in India than you will see in a day in New York's Wall Street or London's Cornhill.

Millions dream of winning a lottery so that they will never again need to work. Suggest to them that work is good for them—indeed, a biological necessity, as Hans Selye called it—and they will laugh derisively.

Enjoying Drudgery

In justifying the segregation of enjoyment and work, many assert that drudgery and toil have been humanity's lot for thousands of years. They claim that only in the last forty years, and even then only in a few Western countries, has there been sufficient material affluence to permit a few lucky people the indulgence of enjoying work.

How is it then that in many "primitive" societies, with what we would regard as appalling material conditions, work is enjoyed? Take, for example, the Yequana people who live deep in the Amazon jungle. Their daily lives were portrayed in Jean Liedloff's book *The Continuum Concept*. Struggle, hardship, and material deprivation were their daily lot. Yet they didn't see things the way we do. For the Yequana, work was not a distinct compartment of their lives; indeed, their vocabulary lacked a word for work.

On one occasion, Liedloff observed several Yequana men and two Italian adventurers as they struggled with their "work." They were traveling up a river by canoe, but a major waterfall blocked their way. They had no option but to effect a backbreaking portage, a task of several hours. Rocks tore at their flesh as they manhandled the canoe in the buffeting current. The Italians were grim throughout this ordeal. The Yequana men laughed delightedly, as if nothing could be more fun.

Liedloff would often accompany women on the task of fetching water—work that we would certainly regard as drudgery. Several times a day they took a precipitous path down the mountain to a stream. Each carried two or three full gourds on the return trip uphill. Was this a hated chore? No, says Liedloff—a "party mood" always prevailed.

FANCY A LIFE OF CONSTANT LEISURE?

What is going on here? How come the "primitive" Yequana people are able to enjoy their work more than we do ours, even though their working conditions are radically harsher? The answer is simple. For them, their

> We have to begin by realizing that work is a biological necessity. Just as our muscles become flabby and degenerate if not used, so our brain slips into chaos and confusion unless we use it for some work that seems worthwhile to us.... The question is not whether or not we should work, but what kind of work suits us best.
>
> *Hans Selye*

> All animals, except man, know that the principal business of life is to enjoy it—and they do enjoy it as much as man and other circumstances will allow.
>
> *Samuel Butler*

work has meaning. The link between the tasks they perform today and the food they eat tomorrow is clear. Working is as central to being alive as breathing.

And what about us? Why do we work? To buy necessities, you might say. Yes, that is true, though our concept of "necessities" is expansive indeed compared with that held by most of the world's population. But we work for many other reasons as well: to win a prestigious promotion; to buy a third television or a new fashion accessory; to redecorate the bathroom; to take an overseas vacation. Good reasons, all of them, by the criteria of a materialistic society—but none of them has much to do with staying alive. They relegate work to a peripheral, functional purpose instead of a central, life-affirming purpose.

It need not be so, not even in the affluent West. The way to bring enjoyment back into work is to reunite work and leisure. You do that by working on something that has intrinsic meaning to your life, in the same way that collecting water has meaning to the lives of the Yequana.

Hans Selye points to Pablo Casals, Winston Churchill, Haile Selassie, Albert Schweitzer, George Bernard Shaw, Henry Ford, Charles de Gaulle, Bertrand Russell, Queen Victoria, Titian, Voltaire, Bismarck, Michelangelo, Pablo Picasso, Henri Matisse, Arthur Rubenstein, Arturo Toscanini, and others. In devoting their lives to their respective callings, all worked extraordinarily hard. All of them struggled, sweated, battled fear and frustration as they went about their life's work. They needed to muster enormous strength and discipline to overcome the barriers confronting them. But, says Selye, "None of them ever 'worked' at all, in the sense of work as something one has to do to earn a living but does not enjoy. Despite their lives of intense activity, they lived a life of constant leisure by always doing what they liked to do."

Once you are in *your* calling, you too will discover the enjoyment that comes from living "a life of constant leisure."

The secret of success is making your vocation your vacation.

Mark Twain

Mahatma Gandhi was once asked, "You have been working at least fifteen hours a day, every day for almost fifty years. Don't you think it's time you took a vacation?" To which Gandhi replied, "I'm always on vacation."

Jon Kabat-Zinn

BEYOND FUN

When talking recently to Teresa, a sales trainee, I asked her if she enjoyed her work. "Parts of it," she replied. "I don't much like the selling side. But it's a good crowd of people who work here, and the social club is active, and I have developed some good friendships." This was enough for Teresa—she planned to stay in sales, even though the core activity of selling left her cold.

Like Teresa, you can mine nuggets of satisfaction out of almost any work environment. But you shouldn't settle for that. Enjoyment should come from the intrinsic nature of the work you are doing, not merely out of peripheral activities like developing friendships with colleagues.

Take Lee, a tennis professional, for example. The core activity of his career is coaching. For him it's great fun, and he is good at it. Skill plus enjoyment is a big advance on skill alone.

But even for Lee, something is missing. "It's fun, but somehow it's not enough," he said to me. The missing dimension? Meaning. When your work activities have meaning, the fun intensifies into something much more profound: bliss.

Old Tom had it wrong. He should have looked on the golfing greats not as cheats but as role models. They honored, not violated, the rules of life. They chose to found their working lives on an activity that they not only excelled at but also enjoyed and valued. By following their bliss, they put their outer lives in tune with the inner promptings of their heart and soul.

Which is what you too need to do if you are to find your calling.

I want to be thoroughly used up when I die. For the harder I work the more I live.

George Bernard Shaw

SEVEN

Meaning

DUD: Yes, but think of all the happy times you've had. That's what I do when I'm feeling below par. This room is filled with joyous memories. Look at this. A certificate proving we've been up the Post Office Tower.
PETE: And why did we go up it?
DUD: Because it was there, Pete, a challenge.
PETE: A brief escape from a life consisting of cups of tea, interminable games of Ludo and the occasional visit to your Aunt Dolly.

PETER COOK AND DUDLEY MOORE

THE WILL TO MEANING

You may not know it, but you're religious.

You may be a Christian or a Jew, a Muslim or a Hindu, a Buddhist or a Jain or a Zoroastrian. You may be an agnostic or an atheist. You may indeed revel in your atheism and proclaim it proudly to all the world. It doesn't matter: You're religious. You belong to the species called *Homo sapiens,* and being religious is part of your biological inheritance.

What does it mean to be religious? The word *religion* has its roots in two Latin words: *re,* meaning

Into this Universe, and why not knowing,
Nor whence, like Water willy-nilly flowing:
And out of it, as Wind along the Waste
I know not Whither, willy-nilly blowing.

Omar Khayyám

55

One does not have to be especially spiritual to experience awe at the infinity of galaxies we see in the night sky. Our human consciousness does not merely make possible the question *Why?* It insists that the question be asked. The urge to know is a defining feature of humanity: to know about the past; to understand the present; to glimpse what the future may hold.

Richard Leakey

"back," and *ligio,* meaning "linking." Linking back. That's what religion is about—linking our lives with what has gone before.

And why are we concerned to do that? It flows out of that extraordinary phenomenon, human consciousness. Our consciousness renders us aware of our predicament: We are microscopic creatures who are doomed to die; and while we await our death we are transported on a ball of fire, water, and rock through a universe of unfathomable vastness. Being aware of that, we want to understand. Why are we here? What do our lives mean? We *need* to understand. And so we are religious.

Viktor Frankl spent many years in Nazi concentration camps and observed how some prisoners coped with unspeakable horror. He concluded that "happiness cannot be pursued; it must ensue." By this he meant that happiness is a by-product. It results from leading a life that has meaning, and hence can occur even in an Auschwitz. Those prisoners in Auschwitz who believed that their existence had meaning coped and, in the end, triumphed over their oppressors.

Frankl, a psychologist, became convinced that our search for meaning is the primary motivation in our lives. He called it "the will to meaning." His wartime experiences led him to endorse Friedrich Nietzsche's words: "He who has a *why* to live for can bear with almost any *how.*"

DO YOU HAVE A *WHY* TO LIVE FOR?

In the good old days, it was easy to be religious. You just took a ready-made faith off the shelf and adopted it as your own. It provided you with an interpretation of life and told you what your individual existence meant in the overall scheme of things.

But in the developed world over the past two hundred years, science and education have rather spoiled the party. As Ernest Becker put it, the appeal of traditional religions rested on mystery, naive belief, simple-minded hope. Science has now furnished explanations of our origins that reduce the mystery, and education has banished naïveté and simple-mindedness. As a result, *Homo sapiens* has been "disinherited by his own analytical strength."

Today, it is fashionable to ridicule the disturbing question of meaning, to pretend that it is an irrelevancy with which only the soft-headed torment themselves. But it is hard to regard Mahatma Gandhi, for example, as soft-headed. In the words of biographer Louis Fischer, "Gandhi sat, so to speak, in a marketplace crisscrossed by tens of millions of persons with their carts, cares, wares, and thoughts, but he sat still and within him there was peace." That peace, and with it his remarkable influence, flowed from his ruthless and courageous commitment to searching out and honoring his own inner truths. The same is true of the Dalai Lama: His extraordinary strength, clarity, joy, and serenity result from facing up to, not running away from, his will to meaning throughout a lifetime of turmoil and dispossession.

By contrast, look closely at those who, suffering from the modern-day malaise that Frankl called the "existential vacuum," purport to revel in the meaninglessness of life. Their innate will to meaning being frustrated, they seek to compensate by substituting what Frankl called "a will to power, including the most primitive form of the will to power, the will to money. In other cases the place of the frustrated will to meaning is taken by the will to pleasure" (by which Frankl meant shallow, hedonistic pleasure). Their lives, compared to Gandhi's and the Dalai Lama's, are rootless and joyless.

How about you? If the traditional faiths no longer satisfy your will to meaning, you too may be a victim of the existential vacuum, living in a desolate wasteland,

> One should not search for an abstract meaning of life. Everyone has his own specific vocation or mission in life to carry out a concrete assignment which demands fulfillment. Therein he cannot be replaced, nor can his life be repeated. Thus, everyone's life is as unique as is his specific opportunity to implement it.
>
> *Viktor Frankl*

From "The Full Alex" published by Headline. Reprinted with permission of Peattie & Taylor.

afflicted with a sense of meaninglessness, blindly pursuing power or pleasure or security.

Unless you create your own meanings. Packaged faiths are not the only source of meaning. You can satisfy your will to meaning by creating your own. That is what you—each of us—must do to escape the spiritual wasteland.

Don't bother asking yourself the question, *What is the meaning of life?* Instead, the question you must tackle is, *What is the meaning of* my *life?* You are unique. Nobody has been, or will be, exactly like you. You will lead a healthy and fulfilling life in proportion to the extent to which you live out what Carl Jung called your "innate idiosyncrasy." Only you can determine what has ultimate meaning for you.

So what does have ultimate meaning for you? Sounds like a heavy question, doesn't it? But it isn't really.

THE FIRST DIMENSION OF MEANING: SELF-ASSERTION

I no longer ask the young man's question, "How far will I go?" My questions now are those of the mature person, "When it is over, what will my life have been about?"

Harold Kushner

Meaning has two dimensions. Both are concerned with making you believe that your life matters, and thereby reducing your sense of insignificance and vulnerability. The first involves assertion of self. The second involves submission of self.

In a sense, the whole of this book is about the first dimension, assertion of self. You need to give expression to what has meaning for your Core Self. That is to be found by exploring (see part 3).

Joseph Campbell's passion, as we saw in chapter 2, was mythology. Peter Scott's was observing and painting geese on the wing. What's yours? Your task in life—your calling—is to realize your potential in the domains where your bliss is to be found. This involves asserting yourself, pushing out the limits of your uniqueness, becoming, to the fullest extent possible, what you are capable of becoming as an individual.

A meaningful life flows from converting potentialities into realities. As Frankl wrote, it is only potentialities that are truly transitory. If not realized, they are "condemned to nonbeing." But if realized, they are "rescued and preserved from transitoriness." The result is that the person who attacks life actively has no reason in old age to envy young people for the life possibilities lying ahead of them. "'No, thank you,'" he will think. "'Instead of possibilities, I have realities in my past, not only the reality of work done and of love loved, but of sufferings bravely suffered.'"

> There are two parallel tasks in spiritual life. One is to discover selflessness, the other is to develop a healthy sense of self, to discover what is meant by true self.
>
> *Jack Kornfield*

THE SECOND DIMENSION OF MEANING: SELF-SUBMISSION

You can reduce your perception of your own puniness by self-assertion, growing in the direction of your potentialities. But you can also do so by self-submission, allowing yourself to become absorbed in something larger than yourself. This involves identifying with something that transcends the temporal limits of your own distinct being.

One way of doing this, of course, is to submit to the

> When someone asks, "What do you think is the meaning of life?" I might answer: Life is an experience and an opportunity. The meaning comes from what we decide to do with the opportunity that is given to us.
>
> *Bernie Siegel*

teachings of certain faiths: for example, the Christian teaching of everlasting life or the Buddhist teaching of reincarnation. But you are a creature of your times, and so your critical faculties may make it hard for you to accept such teachings.

If that is so, identify instead with the mysterious energy that informs the universe. It is manifest in the movement of the stars, the pounding waves of the ocean, the fluttering wings of the butterfly, the cells that first started quivering with life billions of years ago, and the creatures of unknown form to be born in eons to come. It is manifest in you, too. Your life is an expression of that eternal energy source; it is part of you, and you are part of it. You are linked to infinity.

THE RIPPLING POND

"True spirituality," writes Tibetan monk Sogyal Rinpoche, "is to be aware that if we are interdependent with everything and everyone else, even our smallest, least significant thought, word, and action have real consequences throughout the universe. Throw a pebble into a pond. It sends a shiver across the surface of the water. Ripples merge into one another and create new ones. Everything is inextricably interrelated."

If you find Tibetan monks unpersuasive, try Albert Einstein. The cutting edge of physics is quantum mechanics, which studies the behavior of subatomic particles. Einstein and other leading physicists working in this arcane field have developed theories that astonishingly lend weight to the Buddhist and Hindu idea of interconnectedness. In *The Dancing Wu Li Masters*, Gary Zukav summarizes what quantum theory implies: "All of the things in our universe (including us) that appear to exist independently are actually parts of one all-encompassing organic pattern, and . . . no parts of that

So what is this mind, what are these atoms with consciousness? Last week's potatoes! . . . The thing which I call my individuality is only a pattern or dance. The atoms come into my brain, dance a dance, then go out; always new atoms but always doing the same dance, remembering what the dance was yesterday.

Richard Feynman
(Nobel Prize–winning physicist)

pattern are ever really separate from it or from each other."

Picture, then, the ripples that make you who you are. They come out of your past. Think of the nameless ancestor who, ten thousand years ago, gave birth to another of your ancestors. Without her, you would not be here. See how the ripples from her apparently anonymous life continue to reverberate. What ripples are you in turn now sending off into the future? Think of the people you love. Each of them has touched your life, has contributed to making you who you are. You have touched their lives, too. As a result of knowing you, they are different people, and those differences are manifest in the way they act toward others. And so their children, for example, will be affected, and, in time, their children's children. And on and on it goes.

The American psychologist and philosopher William James once said that the greatest use of life is to create something that outlasts it. Your first instinct may be to think it would be presumptuous, indeed arrogant, to suppose that you could create something that outlasts you. Think again. You don't need to do something that makes you famous: to paint a masterpiece, lead a nation, or discover a star. The ripple effect makes it certain that your life, no matter how humble, will have impacts that will endure beyond your passing.

> Life has always seemed to me like a plant that lives on its rhizome. Its true life is invisible, hidden in the rhizome. The part that appears above ground lasts only a single summer. Then it withers away—an ephemeral apparition. When we think of the unending growth and decay of life and civilization, we cannot escape the impression of absolute nullity. Yet I have never lost a sense of something that lives and endures beneath the eternal flux. What we see is the blossom, which passes. The rhizome remains.
>
> *Carl Jung*

WHERE THE TWO DIMENSIONS OF MEANING MEET IN YOU

Self-assertion and self-submission. At first glance, they are in conflict. But it need not be so.

If you believe that you were created by God and that your task on earth is to devote your life to God's service (self-submission), it is your duty to celebrate your uniqueness as a gift from God and, to the best of

> When Matisse was asked whether he believed in God, his response was, "Yes, when I'm working."
>
> *Marion Woodman*

your abilities, turn your unique potentialities into realities (self-assertion).

If you believe that you are inextricably bonded to the wondrous energy force that drives the universe (self-submission), it is your duty to be true to the natural forces within you and develop your unique natural endowments to the utmost (self-assertion).

If you believe that your life is part of an intricate rippling web spanning the universe (self-submission), it is your duty to grow into what you are capable of being so that those ripples are as positive and beneficent as possible (self-assertion).

In any view, the best way to show respect for that to which you choose to submit is to assert yourself by following your bliss. It is through your calling that you can reconcile self-assertion and self-submission.

We come back, then, to you and your working life, and why it matters whether you have a career or a calling. A career frustrates the primal drive within you, the will to meaning. It demands that you assert not yourself as you truly are, but a corrupted version, one that aims to meet social expectations in defiance of the drives residing in the unique organism that is you.

Contrast that with what happens if you are in your calling. Then you deploy the very essence of your being in the service of that which to you is of ultimate meaning. By following your bliss, you breathe life into yourself. And not only that. You also (as we shall see in chapter 23) breathe life into humanity.

This is the true joy in life, the being used for a purpose recognized by yourself as a mighty one; the being a force of nature instead of a feverish selfish little clod of ailments and grievances complaining that the world will not devote itself to making you happy.

George Bernard Shaw

EIGHT

Integration

It is not the child, but only the adult, who can achieve personality as the fruit of a full life directed to this end. The achievement of personality means nothing less than the optimum development of the whole individual human being.

CARL JUNG

WALKING THE HIGH WIRE

Karl Wallenda was a tightrope walker—perhaps the twentieth century's leading exponent of that perilous art. Such was his skill that he became a legend in his own time.

In 1978, Karl Wallenda walked the high wire once too often. While traversing a wire thirty yards above the ground in San Juan, Puerto Rico, he lost balance and plunged to his death.

Serves him right for choosing such a dangerous pursuit, you may be thinking. But don't be too hard on him. For if you're in a career, you're probably a tightrope walker, too.

63

THE THREE CIRCLES OF WORK

We have seen that you have an innate drive to realize the potentialities that comprise your Core Self, and that such drive arises in three dimensions: skill, enjoyment, and meaning. These three dimensions can be represented as three circles, like these:

Living beings have organization. . . . Their function depends entirely on their organization, their mutual interrelations, interactions, and interdependencies.

Ernst Mayr
(biologist)

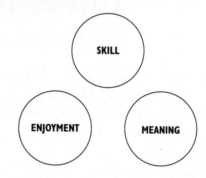

Each circle is shown above as free floating and independent of the others. But is this depiction accurate?

Consider first the dimensions of enjoyment and meaning. There are countless activities that you find fun but that have no meaning for you; others that have meaning but aren't fun. Others still connect with your Core Self and therefore are both enjoyable and meaningful. So let's rearrange the three circles:

Interconnectedness is a fundamental principle of nature. Nothing is isolated. Each event connects with others.

Jon Kabat-Zinn

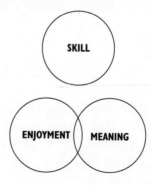

Now what about skill? The universe of activities that you have the skills (actually or potentially) to perform competently is huge. Most of these provide neither enjoyment nor meaning. But some provide enjoyment, others meaning. And a few, your highest talents, express your Core Self and so have the potential to provide both enjoyment and meaning. The three circles thus need to be rearranged again so that all interlock:

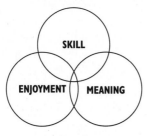

Now comes the key question, one that you cannot avoid answering. Where in relation to these circles are you going to base your working life?

DRAWING A BLANK

You could, if sufficiently masochistic, place yourself right outside the three circles at point A, doing work you neither enjoy nor value nor are capable of doing well.

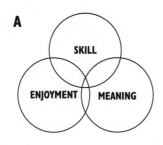

Each of them [Jesus, St. Augustine, St. Francis, Roger Bacon, Charles Darwin, Albert Einstein] in his own tempo and with his own voice discovered and reaffirmed with astonishment the knowledge that all things are one thing and that one thing is all things—plankton, a shimmering phosphorescence on the sea and spinning planets and the expanding universe, all bound together by the elastic string of time.

John Steinbeck and
Edward F. Ricketts

If your current work is devoid of enjoyment and meaning, you may feel that this is the place where you are right now. But beware of jumping to this conclusion too readily. Your angst may be leading you astray: By feeding your insecurity, it may be causing you to underrate your skill.

THE WALLENDA CAREER

One step up from being right outside all three circles is to be within just one of them, at point B:

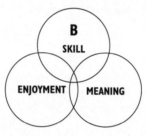

Point B marks a spot that most angst sufferers know only too well. They have the skills to be competent at what they do, but their work lacks both enjoyment and meaning. Since they are relying on skills alone, coping with their working lives is a perilous matter of balance. In effect, they are walking the high wire just like Wallenda. No matter how well an objective bystander might rate their performance, they always feel unworthy and anxious—in a word, *insecure*.

If walking the high wire is inherently hazardous, doing so while fearing failure (which is what insecurity amounts to) makes it even more so. Before one of his tightrope walks, Wallenda was seized by an uncharacteristic fear of failure. In his wife's words (quoted in Warren Bennis's book *Leaders*), "All Karl thought about

By American standards, I was an outstanding success. I looked around and saw two beautiful Mercedes, an elegant home, and a net worth in millions, and yet I was more insecure and filled with self-doubt than I had ever been in my life.

Dennis Augustine

for three straight months prior to it was *falling*. It was the first time he's ever thought about that, and it seemed to me that he put all his energies into *not falling* rather than walking the tightrope." You will not be surprised to learn that this was the walk that claimed his life.

A career that relies on skill alone will in the end cost *you* your life, too. Not literally, of course, but in the sense that you will die to most of the life possibilities within you that would be realized if only you followed your bliss. And so you will live out your years with resignation and a growing sense of lost opportunities.

Two Out of Three Ain't Bad

Being at points A or B makes angst a certainty. Now let's consider points C and D.

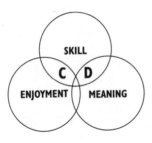

At both of these points you are looking a lot safer than Wallenda. Instead of relying on skill alone, you are sustained as well by either enjoyment (point C) or meaning (point D). But you remain highly vulnerable.

If you're at point C, the absence of meaning has the result that your work fails to connect fully with your Core Self and therefore seems, despite all the fun, to be rather shallow, maybe even hedonistic. This sense of superficiality grows as the years roll by, leading to an increasing sense of emptiness.

Something more unsettling and more tragic than dying frightens us. We are afraid of never having lived, of coming to the end of our days with the sense that we were never really alive, that we never figured out what life was about. . . .

Virtually the only people I have known who were afraid of dying were people who thought that they had wasted their lives.

Harold Kushner

What is needed is to learn afresh, to observe, and to discover for ourselves, the meaning of wholeness.

David Bohm

If you're at point D, the absence of enjoyment means that your work, worthy as it may be, is grim and stressful. Melanie, for example, is a nurse who for four years worked in the emergency ward of a busy metropolitan hospital. Highly competent and well regarded by her superiors and peers, she took great pride in the knowledge that her work helped save lives. There was only one problem: She hated the nonstop gore and trauma. Eventually, she suffered a breakdown. After extensive counseling, she came to see that the enjoyment of work was not a selfish need but a biological necessity.

HITTING THE JACKPOT

Part of being a healthy person is being well integrated and at peace, with all of the systems acting together.

Professor Candace Pert (Center for Molecular and Behavioral Neuroscience, Rutgers University)

Where is your calling? It's not located within just one circle. It is not even to be found where two circles link. Your calling is where all three circles interlock, at point X:

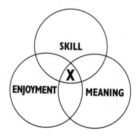

Here your balance is not precarious. In addition to having the skills, you enjoy your work. And on top of that, your work has real meaning. It's the jackpot: three out of three.

BEING HEALTHY AND BEING WHOLE

Heal. Health. Holistic. Whole. All have the same linguistic root: the old Germanic word *hailaz,* meaning "whole."

That bronzed hunk you often see pounding the streets probably thinks of himself as the personification of health. Like so many in our society, he makes the mistake of looking upon health as a physical thing. In worshiping his body, he confuses what is merely a fragment of his being for the real thing.

You are *not* your body. (And just as well, too, because your body is decaying even as you read these words.) The fact is that you are your body plus a lot more besides: a complex of body, mind, emotion, and spirit. And health is a property of this whole person.

What kind of working life, then, is healthy? A calling, because it expresses your Core Self along not just one, not just two, but all three of the vital dimensions. Unlike a career, which simply keeps your body and your ego fed, a calling nourishes your whole being.

So go for the jackpot: skill plus enjoyment plus meaning. Follow your calling, heal your angst, and be whole.

Together the chimpanzees and the baboons and monkeys, the birds and insects, the teeming life of the vibrant forest, the stirrings of the never still waters of the great lake, and the uncountable stars and planets of the solar system formed one whole. All one, all part of the great mystery. And I was part of it too. A sense of calm came over me. More and more often I found myself thinking, "This is where I belong. This is what I came into this world to do."

Jane Goodall

The Process

NINE

Exploration

You can't expect insights, even the big ones, to suddenly make you understand everything. But I figure: Hey, it's a step if they leave you confused in a deeper way.

JANE WAGNER

REVERTING TO TODDLERHOOD

You used to do it. You did it as a baby. As an infant you excelled. You kept on doing it, though with growing inhibition, right through childhood and adolescence. But now you're an adult, and perhaps do it only rarely.

You peaked when you were a toddler. Picture yourself as a two-year-old. You were at a friend's birthday party. You had never been to this house before. It looked kind of interesting. You escaped from the party room and acquainted yourself with every other room in the house. You set about liberating the contents of drawers and cupboards. All in thirty-five seconds flat.

This is called exploring.

Another thing you did was familiarize yourself with the dining table. You did this not by contemplating it,

All life is an experiment. The more experiments you make the better.

Ralph Waldo Emerson

wondering about it, theorizing about it, but by *acting*. If you saw something on a plate that looked vaguely appetizing, you reached out a sticky hand, picked it up, licked it, chomped it, sniffed it, squeezed it, dismembered it. If you found it agreeable, you finished it; if you didn't, you discarded it and moved eagerly on.

This is called experimenting.

Exploring and experimenting—that's how you gained insight into the world and into yourself. It's how you learned to eat, walk, talk, play, write, think, love . . . indeed, it's how you learned to be a human being.

Contrary to popular belief, there is no law against exploring and experimenting in adulthood. Columbus did it. Galileo did it. Even Archimedes in his bath did it. Let's do it. Let's explore and experiment.

> The illiterate of the future will not be the person who cannot read. It will be the person who cannot learn.
>
> *Alvin Toffler*

Because to get from here (angst-ridden, alienated from your Core Self, blind to your potential, cut off from your calling) to there (blissfully following your calling), you need insight—insight into what your skills are, insight into what you truly enjoy, insight into what has special meaning for you.

How can you generate such insight? By reviving your childhood passion for exploring and experimenting. Another way of putting this is that you need to accumulate experiences. Through experiences you learn about your strengths and weaknesses, likes and dislikes, passions and fears; you learn what truly matters to you and what counts for naught.

THE OTHER WAY

There is another way to learn about yourself.

What you do is this: You wait. You wait for insight to come to you out of the ether in a flash of blinding illumination. Or you wait for your fairy godmother to arrange for a stranger to present you with a wonderful opportunity you never dared hope for. Or, if of a more proactive disposition, you plonk yourself down in a comfortable recliner with pen and paper (television volume turned down of course) and wait for solutions to emerge from a vigorous eleven-minute bout of rational problem solving.

This way is highly popular. Pity it never works.

> If you keep on doing what you've always done, you'll keep on getting what you've always got.
>
> *Larry Wilson*

EXPLORING WORKS

Michael majored in accounting. On graduation, he and his best friend, Jim, joined an accounting firm. By the age of twenty-four, both knew two things about being an accountant. First, it was something at which they could become highly skilled if they persevered. Second, it was something that gave them, and would always give them, little joy.

"Have it your way . . . we'll stay here and wait for an African continent to sail past."

Jim was a solid, sensible sort of guy. He knew that work wasn't meant to be enjoyed. So he chose to tough it out. And this worked for him. Now he's a well-respected partner. Okay, so he's miserable, but he *is* a partner—and well off, too. Hey, you can't have everything.

Michael, on the other hand, decided to explore. Over the next fifteen years he worked for an international food company, a health-care insurer, and a sporting goods distributor. Compared with Jim's, his income climbed slowly, but he gained experience in finance, marketing, information technology, and operations management.

During these years of exploring, Michael learned many things—for example, that he liked variety; that he enjoyed taking risks and trying unconventional approaches; that he hated rules and regulations; that he was good at coming up with practical solutions to problems but poor at implementing them; that he was adept at getting along with people; that he treasured his autonomy. And he learned that he had a passion for the world of computers.

When the chance came to buy a boutique computer software store with a friend, Michael took it without hesitation. Now, three years later, he has no regrets, even though the store has been only a moderate success financially. He is thinking of selling his interest in the store within the next couple of years, and has other ideas in the high-tech field that he is investigating. Financially he is worth only half as much as Jim. But unlike Jim, he knows himself well. As a result, he feels secure, happy, fulfilled, confident, and excited about the future.

What Michael did was explore. Exploring works. Paul Evans and Fernando Bartolomé (from INSEAD, one of Europe's leading business schools) carried out extensive research to identify factors that separated managers who, in their forties and fifties, felt fulfilled in their working lives from those who didn't. They identi-

> I'd rather regret the things I've done than the things I have not.
>
> *Lucille Ball*

> You cannot fail at being yourself. A cat doesn't try to be a tiger, and you shouldn't try to be something you aren't. You are a process, not a product. Your job is to discover what you are and to create that creature. You still won't be perfect, but success isn't about perfection—it is about authenticity.
>
> *Bernie Siegel*

fied three common mistakes in launching a career. One was being dazzled by external rewards; another was inability to resist organizational pressures. And the third key mistake—here's the one that matters for now—was insufficient exploration.

The research showed that many managers driven by a desire to climb the career ladder failed to explore. They regarded lateral moves or retraining as time wasted. Through their twenties and early thirties, their career paths tended to be smooth, rapid, outwardly successful. But then their lack of exploration began to catch up with them. Many came to feel that they had made narrow and confining choices. Not having explored other areas, however, they lacked a sense of alternatives or the skills for other jobs. As they entered their forties, such managers often disliked their work but could see no way out.

Contrast the managers who, at the outset of their careers, took several years to explore. They were prepared to make lateral moves to broaden their experience of different disciplines, industries, or organizations. In the short term, this came at a price: They made slower progress up the ladder. But through their exploration, they discovered the work situations that best fitted their personalities. By gaining greater self-knowledge and broader skills, they became far more likely to find a fulfilling work situation from their midthirties onward.

> [The] younger managers in particular think less about what they enjoy doing and value doing. Doing a task badly is taken as an incentive to try to do better next time, not as a reason at least to ask the question: "Do I really want to have a job involving that kind of work, and do I really value it?"
>
> *Paul Evans and*
> *Fernando Bartolomé*

THE EXPLORATION CYCLE

Exploration is a cycle. You reflect on your experiences to learn more about yourself; you bring about changes to create new experiences and the opportunity for new learning; you expose yourself to those new experiences; you reflect further; and so on.

> We cannot teach people anything; we can only help them discover it within themselves.
>
> *Galileo*

REFLECT

EXPERIENCE

CHANGE

Reflecting

The purpose of reflecting is to glean insight from your experiences. Others may be able to judge how good you are at an activity, but only you can know how an experience affects you inside, and in particular whether it touches an activity in your Core Self.

Reflection has to be, in large measure, a solitary, contemplative exercise. Disciplines like meditation, to be discussed later (see pages 162–163), help. But outsiders can help, too. A mentor or a counselor can prod you onward by asking questions, making observations, and drawing insights out of you. Family members, friends, and colleagues—anyone who knows you well in a particular context—can point out things that are so obvious you don't see them yourself.

Charles Handy tells of an account director at an advertising agency who was laid off. At Handy's suggestion, he asked twenty friends and colleagues to tell him just one thing he did well. He then came back to Handy. "I've got a list of twenty things," he said. "Quite surprising, some of them. Funny thing, though—none of them mentioned running an account group."

Personality tests such as the Myers-Briggs Type Indicator may help your reflection, too. These never lie. Even if they are wrong, they are right, for they simply

O wad some Pow'r the
giftie gie us
To see oursels as others
see us!

Robert Burns

reveal how you see yourself. The results are often illuminating. They provide further clues—information to put in the pot, along with all the other information you are collecting—to help you interpret your experiences and determine what changes to make.

Changing and Experiencing

The learning derived from your reflection will lead you toward change. Why make a change? So that you can have some new experiences, thereby beginning the whole exploration cycle afresh.

As an explorer, you seek to effect not momentous change in one fell swoop, but rather an accumulation of small changes. With this mind-set, you can discern myriad possibilities for new experiences, both at work and away from work.

There will, of course, be times in your exploration when you need to make a truly significant change, like resigning to take up a new job or to embark on further study. But here's the point: Such a move need not and should not be a leap into the dark. If it is preceded by appropriate, and if necessary prolonged, experimenting and reflecting, then it can be undertaken at relatively low risk.

> If it fails, admit it frankly, and try another. But above all, try something.
>
> *Franklin Delano Roosevelt*

THE SPIRAL CAREER

On the traditional linear approach to careers, you embark on a particular career early in life and stick with it until retirement. In its purest form, you stick not merely with the same career but with the same company. Your goal, to be achieved over forty-odd years, is to climb from the bottom rung as far up the ladder as you can get. Each new rung brings more prestige and added material rewards. The prospect of advancement, rather than intrinsic rewards, is what fuels your ambi-

> Do you know what depression is? It's when you have spent your whole life climbing the corporate or whatever kind of ladder and you finally reach the top and find it's against the wrong wall.
>
> *Joseph Campbell*

tion. Once upon any rung, you devote your energies to doing whatever will get you to the next rung.

The trouble is, you may think you're climbing a ladder, but in truth you're penetrating a canyon. With every year that passes, you further subjugate facets of your Core Self. As your life narrows, the canyon walls become ever higher. They tower over you by the time you reach middle age. It can then seem that escape is impossible, that you have no option but to keep trudging onward along the floor of the canyon until rescued by retirement.

> Only the wisest and stupidest of men never change.
>
> *Confucius*

If you become an explorer, you may find yourself on what is called a spiral career path. This is an apt name because, given the repetitive nature of the exploration cycle (experience, reflect, change; experience, reflect, change), exploring is best seen as a spiral. With each cycle, you learn more about yourself. As you learn, so you and your life move onward. Over time, major shifts in direction can be effected.

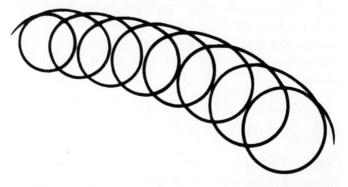

> Progress never moves in a straight line. It's a spiral pathway, now going, now returning, holding on and letting go, winning and losing, giving and receiving.
>
> *Dennis Augustine*

The spiral career consists of successive careers that may differ qualitatively from each other. Yet some continuity is maintained because each career builds on what has been learned in previous ones.

To start on a spiral career path, you find an area of work that interests you. For several years you remain in that area, though not necessarily in the same job. But as

time goes by, you grow, your interests and aptitudes evolve, and gradually you come to feel that your current career no longer fits the person that you now are. One day you feel ready to try something different, and so you launch yourself into a new career. You remain there for so long as it fits, then once again move on.

A spiral career can liberate you from the linear career canyon. Suddenly the questions you face seem less momentous. No longer are they, *Do I jettison career A and adopt career B? Is this feasible? Is it desirable? What if career B proves as joyless for me as career A? What if I fail in career B?* Rather, they are, *What have I learned about myself from career A? What might I learn about myself if I spend a few years in career B? Might it steer me toward my calling? And would it be fun to try?*

> Jump into experience while you are alive.... What you call "salvation" belongs to the time before death.
>
> *Kabir*

THE EXPLORER'S MIND-SET

Are you a tourist? A tourist likes to visit places. It's the places that count; the journey to get there is a necessary evil—something to be endured, not enjoyed.

If you are stuck in a career that is not working for you, you are probably a tourist. You don't like your current job. You spend a lot of time pondering on other possible jobs. Your criteria are perfectly reasonable. All you want is a new job in which you will be blissfully happy, which will provide as much or more status and pay, and which starts next Monday. When no such job materializes, you stay where you are, or flit to another job that is substantially the same but has the virtue of being easy to come by. And then, you whine that it's no better than the job you left.

If you want to find your calling, you must become an explorer. As such, you have a radically different mind-set. You do not shrink from change—far from it, you move out to welcome it. You relish the process of self-discovery. It's the getting there, not the arrival, that you love.

> Life is guided by a changing understanding of and interpretation of my experience. It is always in process of becoming.
>
> *Carl Rogers*

Being an Aircraft Carrier

"All will be well," many people say, "if only I can get a new career/job/spouse/car/hairdo . . ." All too often this leads them to make a radical and high-risk change in their lives—a change that soon reveals itself to have been a leap from the frying pan into the fire.

If you have the explorer's mind-set, you won't be tempted to hop from job to job, organization to organization, career to career. Exploring involves, instead, a series of small incremental changes. Like an aircraft carrier, your life needs to be turned around slowly, degree by degree. Changes need not be—usually *should* not be—momentous. It will take five years or more to do all the things needed to put your life on a new course. The question is not whether a particular change will bring about nirvana tomorrow. It is whether it will keep nudging you toward or along the path of your calling.

> True life is lived when tiny changes occur.
>
> *Leo Tolstoy*

The "Stuck Schmuck" Trap

The story is often told of the city slicker who gets lost while driving in the countryside. He seeks directions from a yokel, who, upon hearing of the destination, chews thoughtfully upon a straw before pronouncing, "You can't get there from here."

Don't fall into the trap of believing *I can't get there from here*. Its corollary is *I've wasted a large chunk of my life*. And that belief can lead to endless self-pity and self-flagellation. *What a schmuck I am,* you may find yourself thinking. *I've spent so many years of my life getting to where I am now—and it would be dumb to consign all that to the scrap heap. So I'm stuck where I am.*

The explorer knows that you can *only* get there from here. You are where you are, and the experiences of your career to date deserve to be valued because they are part of bringing you to that point. The journey you now face involves moving forward from that point to others, as yet unknown. And you will find that, in countless ways you cannot foresee, the career you now malign has armed you with skills and knowledge that will prove to be invaluable in whatever turns out to be your calling.

The "Perfect Job" Illusion

If you are tempted to believe that somewhere there exists for you a single "perfect job," and that your task is to find it, you have the mind-set of a tourist. There is no such thing as a "perfect job"—how can there be, when you are a different person today from who you were a year ago, and will be different again in a year's time? But there is something much better: a calling, perhaps more than one. A calling isn't a place. It is a direction. Follow that direction, and you will experience work fulfillment in places more numerous than you can currently imagine.

> Go—not knowing where. Bring—not knowing what. The path is long, the way unknown.
>
> *Russian fairy tale*

"But I Don't Have Time to Explore"

When she first came to see me, Carol, a lively and multitalented twenty-two-year-old, had just been accepted as a trainee teacher. In college, she had (in her own words) "indulged" herself by studying subjects that she truly enjoyed, like art history. But time was running out; she would get "left behind" if she didn't embark on a career quickly. Her friends all had "good jobs and good incomes" already. And her parents had reminded her that the job market was tough and that she had better get some professional qualifications without any more "time-wasting." The "obvious" thing, given her geography major, was to teach geography at a high school. "I just don't have time to explore," she told me.

Carol proved to be one of the lucky ones. It was a tough call, but eventually, after much anguish, she took the time to explore. She declined the trainee teacher position, took up a part-time library position, and helped produce a Spanish-language play. In the ensuing nine years, she explored several domains that interested her. She now lectures in Spanish at college and is writing a book on sixteenth-century Spanish painters. To her, this is bliss.

> It is never too late to be what you might have been.
>
> *George Eliot*

If a twenty-two-year-old can feel that she is running out of time, how much stronger that feeling can be for older people, especially as family and financial commitments mount. Yet the proven correlation between exploration and long-term work fulfillment is strong. That is why Evans and Bartolomé gave to middle-aged adults rejoining the workforce after raising a family the same advice they gave to university graduates: Explore, and be willing to set aside many years to do so.

EXPLORING IN THE REAL WORLD

You know the fable about Icarus. He's the fellow who glued wings to himself and succeeded in flying. But he flew too close to the sun. The glue melted, the wings fell off, and he crashed to his death. Less well known is that Daedalus, Icarus's father, also flew, and did so without mishap. It was Daedalus, in fact, who invented the wings in the first place. He gave his son due warning. If you go too high, he said, the sun will melt the glue. If you go too low, the sea's waves will get you. Fly the middle way. Icarus died because he refused to compromise.

Okay, you have a family to feed; you have children to bring up; you have a mortgage to pay off; you have your old age to provide for. For all these reasons and more, you're going to have to make compromises in your life. That much is clear. But it doesn't follow that you need to forgo exploration. Everyone—*everyone*—has the scope to adopt into his or her life the explorer's mind-set.

Look at the continuum drawn below:

A   B

EXTREME ANGST   PURE BLISS

Your goal as an explorer is not to arrive at Pure Bliss. Pure Bliss, after all, is but an ideal. Rather, your goal is to dedicate the remaining years of your life to moving as far as possible along the continuum toward that ideal. It is to get to B. B is bliss with compromise.

It's well worth shooting for. For all its flaws, B is a thousand times better than A. Because A is angst with excuses and regrets. That will be your lot if you choose not to explore.

> No facts are sacred; none are profane; I simply experiment, an endless seeker, with no past at my back.
> *Ralph Waldo Emerson*

> I always wanted to be somebody, but I should have been more specific.
> *Jane Wagner and*
> *Lily Tomlin*

TEN

Journey

Two roads diverged in a wood, and I—
I took the one less traveled by.
And that made all the difference.

ROBERT FROST

CLICHÉ TIME

Your life is a journey. You've heard it so often, it sounds like Trite Philosophy 101. Still, it happens to be true. If, armed with the explorer's mind-set, you set off in search of life, liberty, and happiness, you will keep traveling for the rest of your days. It's not that you will never find your calling; you will. But by then you will understand that your calling is a direction, not a place. It is a direction, moreover, that constantly leads you to take new directions and find new callings. And so your journey of exploration never ends.

VALUES

If you learned today that you had only a year to live, how would you choose to spend that year? If you had

> Life, at its best, is a flowing, changing process in which nothing is fixed. . . . I find I am at my best when I can let the flow of my experience carry me, in a direction which appears to be forward, toward goals of which I am but dimly aware.
>
> *Carl Rogers*

three days to see, what would you choose to see in those days?

Questions such as these help you identify what really matters to you. They help you identify what you truly value. Which is another way of saying that they help you identify your values.

The word *values* is thrown around a lot these days, and is degraded in the process. If I were to ask you what your values are, you might be inclined to see this as a motherhood-and-apple-pie question, to be answered with a pat set of platitudes. Standard packages are readily available—from your parents, your friends, your church, your workplace, your community, or the media.

But what are the values of your Core Self? These are peculiar to you; only you can determine what they are. And there are no rules or "shoulds" about their content. Even when, genetically, one of your values is like one of mine, each of us will formulate it in our own highly personal way.

It is crucial that you bring these values to your consciousness. This is the labor of a lifetime. It results from exploration and, above all, reflection.

Why is this so important? Because the values of your Core Self are a lodestar that will guide you on your journey. When your working life is in harmony with those values, then you will know that you have found your calling.

WINNING THE BIG ONE

Isabel, a thirty-year-old economist, was doing well in her career, yet was miserable. This perplexed her. What was wrong with her?

"Suppose you win the lottery tomorrow," her counselor said. "Suppose you win several million dollars, a sum so large you never again need to worry about earning a living. You are free, absolutely free, for the first

> It is not easy to find happiness in ourselves, but it is not possible to find it elsewhere.
>
> *Agnes Repplier*

> I believe that when your answer to the question of what you would do in the next twelve months is the same whether you have won the lottery or have learned you are going to be dead, then you are really living your life. You are living fully in the moment.
>
> *Bernie Siegel*

time in your life, to forget the dollars and base your work choices entirely on what you would most enjoy. What work will you choose to do?"

Isabel contemplated this question for a minute, then looked up despairingly. "I haven't a clue," she said. "I suppose that once upon a time, when I was a kid, I had passions and hobbies. But I have none now. I simply can't think of anything that I enjoy."

The lottery question frightened Isabel. If you have lost contact with your Core Self, it may frighten you, too. But keep on asking it over and over and over again during your exploration until, dimly at first, then with more clarity, answers begin to emerge.

FINDING THE BLEEDING OBVIOUS

For a long time, your exploring may seem to take you nowhere except around and around in circles. Don't be surprised if what emerges first is a growing sense of what is *not* the right direction. Cherish this: It is a sign that you are making progress.

As your exploration proceeds, you will gradually become more attuned to what your heart and soul are telling you. You will begin to sense that they seem to be pointing to a certain domain or field of endeavor.

John Cleese's most famous character, Basil Fawlty, suggested that his wife Sybil should enter the television quiz show *Mastermind*, having as her specialist subject "the bleeding obvious." That's what your exploring should sooner or later reveal: the bleeding obvious.

Love travel? Become involved with travel. Love politics? Become involved with politics. Love food? Become involved with food. Love helping people? Become involved with helping people. Love books? Become involved with books. Love design? Become involved with design.

Obvious, yes. The simple fact, however, is that the

I observe first that characteristically the client shows a tendency to move away, hesitantly and fearfully, from a self that he is not. . . . And of course in so doing he is beginning to define, however negatively, what he is.

Carl Rogers

world is full of unhappy people whose chosen careers have little to do with what they love. If you're reading this book, you're probably one of them.

What you are looking for is a domain within which to continue your exploring. A domain is simply a field of human interest or endeavor described in the most general of terms. Travel. Politics. Food. Helping people. Books. Design. These are all domains. So are Africa, outer space, beetles, basketball, building bridges, healing, the environment, rhythm and blues. The possibilities are infinite.

So what domain is, for you, the bleeding obvious? The clue, normally, lies in what you enjoy. What do you enjoy doing in your spare time? What do you enjoy reading about? What do you enjoy talking about? What sort of people do you enjoy being with? What would you like to do so much that, if you were filthy rich, you would pay to do it?

Whatever it is, the bleeding obvious won't just be a passing fad, a passion of the moment. It will be something that has stood the test of time, something that was probably evident in your childhood.

DON'T LOOK FOR A DESTINATION

You're an explorer, not a tourist. So you are *not* looking for a specific destination—merely a general domain. If you don't see the distinction, maybe this will help:

Domains	Destinations
Travel	Travel agent. Cashier on cruise boat. Pilot. English-language teacher in Japan. Travel writer.
Politics	Politician. Political scientist. Lobbyist. Press secretary. Political commentator.

> We are having experiences all the time which may on occasion render some sense of this, a little intuition of where your bliss is. Grab it. No one can tell you what it is going to be. You have to learn to recognize your own depth.
>
> *Joseph Campbell*

Food	Chef. Restaurateur. Delicatessen manager. Market gardener. Cookbook writer.
Helping people	Counselor. Family lawyer. Small-business adviser. Hospice worker. Personal fitness coach.
Books	Book retailer. Author. Librarian. Editor. Publisher's accountant.
Design	Interior decorator. Landscape designer. Office manager for architects. Commercial artist. Contributor to design magazines.

What happens if you aim to find a destination rather than a domain? The ghouls representing your fears and self-doubts will have a field day. They'll find any number of ways to knock the particular destination you have in mind. "Join a travel agency? Get real! You have no experience." "Become a politician? You're kidding me. You have the voter appeal of a grass grub." "Give up your profession to become a chef? And confess to failure?" "Become a counselor? Hah! You'll waste years becoming qualified and then decide you don't like it." "Run a bookshop? You'd be bored silly within a month. And broke." "Become a landscape designer? Aren't you a bit old, dearie, to be taking up something new and creative like that?"

And anyway, if you focus on one particular destination, you will inevitably fail to see countless others within the same domain—destinations that may have far more joys to offer you. Edmund Hillary, for example, sensed as a young man that his bliss lay in the mountains. He set off into that domain, without having particular destinations in mind. Had he said as a twenty-year-old, "I want to be the first man to climb Mount Everest. And if I can't do that, I want to have nothing at all to do with the mountains," he would have remained a beekeeper.

The fourth floor of the American Museum of Natural History was the shrine, the principal magic place . . . of my youth. I first visited with my father at age five, and decided right then to dedicate my life to paleontology.

Stephen Jay Gould

As it happens, his pursuit did enable him to conquer Everest. But that achievement was simply a by-product of his exploring his domain. More to the point, his deepest joys have come from activities that did not enter his mind when he was twenty: building schools and hospitals in Nepal.

SETTING OFF INTO YOUR DOMAIN

As you consider which domain to explore further, you may find yourself weighing up several possibilities and agonizing over which to select. Opt for the one that stirs and excites you most, the one that, for some idiosyncratic reason you probably can't explain, seems to matter most to you. You needn't fret that you may be making the "wrong" choice. As long as the domain you focus on holds genuine appeal, then exploring it will move you forward profitably.

Your task now is to find a point of entry, a way to insert yourself into your chosen domain so that you can start learning more about it.

You can begin by putting your nonworking time to better use. You are awake but not at work for around three hundred hours each month: Allocate as many of those as possible to exploring the domain. Become involved, in your spare time, in activities within the domain. Join a club or organization. Talk to friends, acquaintances, contacts who already work in the

> The moment one definitely commits oneself, then Providence moves too. All sorts of things occur to help one that would never otherwise have occurred. A whole stream of events issues from the decision, raising in one's favor all manner of unforeseen incidents and meetings and material assistance, which no man could have dreamed would have come his way.
>
> W. H. Murray

domain. Go to workshops or public presentations. Read books or periodicals.

At the same time, look for opportunities within your current workplace. Your organization may have customers or suppliers who operate within the domain. And it probably offers you the chance to develop skills and knowledge that you could later utilize within the domain.

Eventually you will come to the point where you want to work within the domain. You may be prepared to accept a cut in pay and status if that will get you inside the domain so that you can continue your exploring there. While such a cut amounts to "going backward" by the criteria of the linear career, you are in fact taking a giant step forward by the only criterion that matters: *Will this job lead me away from angst and toward my calling?*

BEING FLEXIBLE AND OPPORTUNISTIC

You have now entered your domain and have found work there. The work may be prosaic, but the point is that now you're in the milieu that fascinates you, possibly for the first time in your working life. You will work with an enthusiasm, even a passion, you have not previously displayed.

Now you have the chance to learn, observe how things work, make contacts, pick up information, build networks, develop skills and knowledge. You also have the chance to impress. If you are in a relatively menial job that makes minimal use of your talents and qualifications, you will probably perform outstandingly. Your performance will be noticed. New responsibilities will be thrown your way, thereby exposing you to still more learning and new contacts. You will be presented with unexpected opportunities from surprising quarters. You are on your way.

> You begin to meet people who are in the field of your bliss, and they open the doors to you. I say, follow your bliss, and don't be afraid, and doors will open where you didn't know they were going to be.
>
> *Joseph Campbell*

CHANGING DIRECTION

Remember the explorer's mind-set. You are a person in the process of becoming. You are flowing, not static. Day by day you are changing, evolving, growing. It follows that you have the freedom to change course, to head for another domain if called to it.

> Any path is only a path, and there is no affront, to oneself or to others, in dropping it if that is what your heart tells you. . . . Look at every path closely and deliberately. Try it as many times as you think necessary. Then ask yourself, and yourself alone, one question . . . Does this path have a heart? If it does, the path is good; if it doesn't it is of no use.
>
> *Carlos Castaneda*

You are like a hiker on a forest trail. You are heading contentedly to the north when you come upon a trail leading off to the northeast. For some reason, this path seems to beckon. So you leave the main trail and take the new one. If it proves to offer even more joys, you don't lament the time "wasted" on the old trail. Not only did the first trail provide its own share of pleasures, but it took you to the point where you had both the opportunity and the impulse to take the new trail.

At the time, you may see no pattern in your changes of direction. But in years to come when you look back, you will see that apparently lucky events and unconnected parts of your life had a coherence to them, combining to ensure that things turned out as they were meant to turn out.

Like the hiker's trail, yours will be a continuous path, even if you change directions from time to time as you head into new domains. You will find that the domains you explore are not distinct, requiring you to leap from one to another like this:

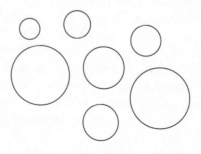

Rather, they will flow one to the other like this:

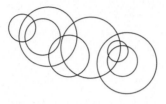

As you progress, you will constantly refine and redefine domains, with each such refinement opening up new possibilities.

FINDING MULTIPLE CALLINGS

Try peeling an onion down to its core. You take one layer off, then another and another. You find the core. Then you realize that you are mistaken: What you are looking at is just another layer. So you peel that layer off, too. Now you've found the core. No, wait, you haven't; it too is just another layer. So you keep peeling layer after layer, getting ever closer to the true core.

That's how your journey of exploration is. You push toward being true to your Core Self, push toward realizing your potential. All the time you are peeling off layers. And what do you find? You find yourself. Or rather, you keep on finding what you think is yourself but then realize that there is more still to find. The discovery that yesterday seemed insightful seems obvious today, flawed and incomplete tomorrow. All the time you are getting closer to your Core Self, closer to your bliss.

Thus it is that over time you may discover, by responding to what is calling you, that you have not one calling but several, each to be undertaken at a different stage of your journey as your being unfolds with the passing years.

There is an interesting verse in the Bible's Book of Revelations: "To anyone who prevails, the Spirit says, I will give you a white stone and on it is written a new name that no one knows save the one to whom it is given." I do not quite know what that means. But I think it means that if at the end of your life you have discovered who you really are and what you are really capable of in the fullness of your being, then you get your real name and your white stone.

Charles Handy

ELEVEN

Ripeness

Ripeness is all.

SHAKESPEARE *(KING LEAR)*

CHANGING LIGHTBULBS

Question: How many psychiatrists does it take to change a lightbulb?
Answer: Only one. But the lightbulb has to really *want* to change.

An old and corny joke, intended of course to mock psychiatrists. They are notorious for suggesting that patients are attached to their problems and don't really want to be rid of them. This suggestion, though usually well founded, can seem absurd as well as insulting to a patient who is sitting there sobbing in pain and misery while forking out two hundred dollars an hour for the privilege.

In reality, the butt of the joke is you. Because if you

are prone to kidding yourself—and who isn't?—then your progress on your journey may well be hampered by delusion: in particular, the delusion that you want to change when you are not yet ready to do so.

THE OVERFLOWING TEACUP

What do you mean, not ready? I can hear you growl. *Of course I'm ready. Things are lousy. I've had enough. I want to change. I'm* committed *to change. Sure I'm ready.*

I'm not convinced.

A Buddhist fable tells of an impatient and somewhat arrogant man on a spiritual quest. He hunts out a sage who he believes can show him the way to enlightenment. "Tell me, Master, what I need to do," he implores. The sage offers him a cup of tea. He holds out his cup and the sage starts pouring. But when the cup is full, the sage doesn't stop. He just keeps on pouring, and of course the cup overflows. The man is a little embarrassed. He doesn't want to offend the sage, but eventually he says, "Excuse me—the cup is full." To which the sage replies, "Yes. Just like your mind. It will need to be emptied before it will be able to receive and hold anything new. Go away, and come back when you are ready."

> When the student is ready, the teacher will appear.
>
> *Anonymous*

Change requires taking on board new learning and a new way of living. It sounds so easy. And it is, once you've made room. Making room—that's the hard part.

Making room involves letting go of things you're currently attached to. What things? Well, habits for a start. Attitudes. Beliefs. Patterns of thinking and behavior. These have been programmed into your brain. When new learning conflicts with an existing program, something has to give. Either the old program has to be altered, or the new learning gets rejected. In the former case, you are ripe for change, and so change takes place.

In the latter case, you are not ripe for change, so nothing changes.

In his book *Mastery,* George Leonard describes the process of learning as explained by Karl Pribram, professor of neuroscience at Stanford University. You have a habitual behavior system that enables you to do things unthinkingly. To learn a new skill, old patterns of sensing, cognition, and movement found within the habitual system need to be replaced. This is achieved by two other systems: the cognitive system and the effort system. These "click into" the habitual system, reprogram it, then withdraw.

> Every education is a kind of inward journey.
>
> *Vaclav Havel*

Hurdles and Plateaus

Wouldn't it be just great if ripeness, in the context of your journey of exploration, was something that you had to achieve just once, like this:

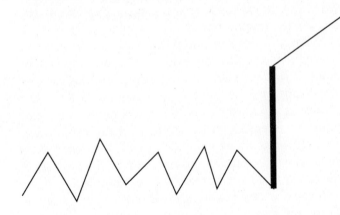

The jagged line represents your life at present. The thick vertical line represents the ripeness hurdle. You're at the foot of it. You have to reprogram, but once you've

> Truth cannot be grasped by the throat like a highwayman's victim, but will reveal itself in its own time.
>
> *John Blofeld*

done that, you're ripe. Then off you go on your journey, heading unstoppably toward nirvana.

But—and this won't surprise you at all—it doesn't happen that way. The way it *really* works is more like this:

There's not just one ripeness hurdle; there are hundreds of them. And after each hurdle you plateau, or even regress. Why is this? Because, if you persevere with your exploration, you keep changing all the time, so the need for reprogramming arises continually.

What you need to do, as Leonard says, is learn to love the plateau. You see, it is not that nothing is happening during the plateau; it is just that nothing *appears* to be happening. Learning is occurring all the time, but it's always up against those old ingrained patterns. Sooner or later, if you persevere with the exploration cycle, reprogramming will take place. Then you will be ripe to cross the hurdle and move on to the next stage of learning, the next plateau, the next hurdle.

If, on the other hand, you become impatient at the plateau and give up, it will be a victory for the old programs of your brain. As long as they endure, they will prevent genuine learning and change from taking place. Much as you may kid yourself that you want to change, you will then be like the foolish fellow with the overflowing teacup.

> As I have struggled with the mystery of my death, seeking the meaning of this life, I have found what I am looking for. It is very simple. We *are* here to learn. Everything that happens to us helps our learning.
>
> M. Scott Peck

MEET THE FLINTSTONES

"There is a time for every purpose under heaven," according to Ecclesiastes. And when it comes to human beings and life realignment, there seems to be a time that is particularly propitious for learning.

That time is middle age. This is when your focus changes. Having spent your twenties and thirties building your place in the world, you find that your energies, previously directed outward, turn to inner concerns. The so-called midlife crisis typically represents a yearning by the Core Self, suffocated by neglect during the years when social concerns were given priority, to be allowed to find expression.

You are the creature of your evolutionary history, and so this desire to turn your attention from building the material things of your outer world to finding meaning in your inner world has primal roots. Put modern life out of your mind for a moment. Consider instead the life for which evolution has equipped you. Send yourself back in time a few thousand years to visit your ancestors. By midlife, their job in terms of the survival of the species was, on the face of it, completed. They had nurtured their children though to independence, thereby ensuring that their genes had been passed to the next generation. And their strength was waning, so that they were less able to make the physical contributions of old.

So why, barring disease, accident, or attack by a rogue mammoth, did they stay alive after that for many decades, consuming resources that would otherwise have been available for their offspring? There has to be a good reason. As Carl Jung observed, "A human being certainly would not grow to be seventy or eighty years old if his longevity had no meaning for the species."

The answer lies in the word *meaning*. As your ancestors grew older, their accumulated experience

> Midway upon the journey
>   of our life
> I found that I was in a
>   dusky wood;
> For the right path, whence
>   I had strayed, was lost.
> Ah me! How hard a thing
>   it is to tell
> The wildness of that rough
>   and savage place,
> The very thought of which
>   brings back my fear!
> So bitter was it, death is
>   little more so.
>
> *Dante*

gave them an enhanced ability to understand, interpret, and find meaning in the world in which they, their family, and their tribe lived. By contributing wisdom to their society, they could further improve the survival odds of their offspring.

RIPENING IN MIDDLE AGE

The Hindus formally recognize, and properly cherish, this contribution of wisdom. They hold that life has four distinct stages: student, householder, seeker, renunciate.

- The student undertakes the formal learning required to live in the material world.
- The householder establishes and maintains a family, and works to create enough wealth to meet the family's material needs.
- Then, at midlife, comes the stage of the seeker. The seeker, like the student, is concerned with learning, though this time the learning relates not to the outer, material world, but to the inner, spiritual world. And like the householder, the seeker is concerned with growth: growth, however, not in material wealth, but in wisdom and understanding.
- The final stage is that of the renunciate who gives up his or her material possessions and communes with God in preparation for dying.

> The crucial innings of the Second Adulthood are neither played by the same rules nor scored in the same way as a young man's game.
>
> *Gail Sheehy*

In Western societies, the primal drive for midlife reorientation is not formally acknowledged, let alone accommodated. But it is there, all right. Around the age of forty your energies can be expected to switch. Your organism will instinctively seek to replace outward concerns—establishing the family, establishing the career—

When Norman awoke one morning,
it suddenly became clear to him:
the time had come to toss aside
his material wealth and look inwards.

with inward concerns as it grapples with such questions as: *Who am I? What is my life about? What is the meaning of it all?*

Whether you are open to this change is another matter altogether. Many resist it. They choose what psychologist Erik Erikson, in his classic book *Childhood and Society,* termed "maintenance," meaning an adherence to the status quo. Erikson called the alternative "generativity," which is in essence a commitment to renewal and growth.

This choice—maintenance or generativity—has potentially chilling consequences. They are well illustrated by the results of the Grant Study, which, starting in 1939 and continuing for several decades, closely

I felt very different and removed from my peers and colleagues. I felt just as if I were going on a long journey, and it would be quite a while, if ever, until I would return to be with them. I walked off into my own world.

Joseph Jaworski

tracked the lives of around 260 American males. The thirty individuals who, in their fifties, represented what were called the "Best Outcomes" (using thirty-two social, psychological, physical, and work-related criteria of health) had all, when faced with midlife turmoil, chosen generativity. The thirty individuals who represented the "Worst Outcomes" had all chosen maintenance.

WHY WAIT?

> The nearer we approach to the middle of life, and the better we have succeeded in entrenching ourselves in our personal attitudes and social positions, the more it appears as if we had discovered the right course and the right ideals and principles of behavior. For this reason we suppose them to be eternally valid, and make a virtue of unchangeably clinging to them. We overlook the essential fact that the social goal is attained only at the cost of a diminution of personality. Many—far too many—aspects of life which should also have been experienced lie in the lumber room among dusty memories; but sometimes, too, they are glowing coals under gray ashes.
>
> *Carl Jung*

Danger lurks in this talk of achieving ripeness in middle age: You could use it to justify procrastination. If your midlife is still some years away, you might say, "Change is impossible unless I am ripe for it. I am clearly not ripe for it now, and I won't be until I reach middle age."

Wrong! Middle age is not a precondition to exploration and life change. It is simply a time when many people who have hitherto denied their Core Selves experience a particularly strong biological impulse to change—an impulse so strong that it causes them to persevere with learning for long enough to enable reprogramming to take place. But a thirty-year-old who perseveres with exploration can achieve reprogramming, too. And it makes sense to do it then. The longer you delay exploration, the harder the task of finding your calling. With every year that passes, more stones are added to the wall of the prison built around your Core Self.

If you are already in your midlife, the pressures to procrastinate are even more pronounced. Hindu society may support seekers, but modern Western society expects you to keep pushing onward in wealth creation during your forties and fifties, notwithstanding that your family may be off your hands and that your material needs may be declining. A trap has been laid for you: a trap that has you accumulating ever more possessions and obligations, instead of accommodating your innate need to turn your attention inward.

To procrastinate at middle age is to choose maintenance over generativity. This path is dangerous. It keeps you trudging deeper and deeper into the high-walled canyon. With each step a little more life is sucked out of you. So you too are in a race against time.

TURNING ON THE LIGHT

Ripeness is not an absolute state, absent one day and then, bingo! present the next. At each stage of learning you ripen imperceptibly. Gradually you achieve a readiness to let go of old patterns, thus empowering yourself to move onward.

It may be only after many years of exploring that, looking back, you realize you have indeed changed. You see that you are now doing things that once you said you could or would never do. You recognize that you have traversed obstacles that once appeared insurmountable. You notice that you have made what once you judged to be unthinkable sacrifices; now they hardly seem to have been sacrifices at all. Previously you were desperate for a quick fix; now you trust that things will happen when they are meant to happen. Previously you were immobilized by the absence of an obvious and achievable destination; now you are happy to be traveling along a trail that is taking you to unknown places.

When you consider your life in retrospect, it seems that you have emerged out of darkness into light. I guess that's what comes of changing the lightbulb.

> Self-knowledge has no end—you don't come to an achievement, you don't come to a conclusion. It is an endless river.
>
> *Krishnamurti*

The Environment

Organizations

*And God created the Organization and
gave It dominion over man.*
—Genesis 1, 30A, Subparagraph VIII

Robert Townshend

Caveat Emptor

You may be there already: inside an organization, in
full-time employment. This is still the place where most
(though a diminishing percentage of) people work. If
you're on the conventional career path, this is almost
certainly where you are right now.

If you're an explorer, you may not be working
inside an organization now, but you probably will be,
sooner or later. Explorers, however, need to beware.
There are organizations and organizations. Some provide a rewarding environment for explorers; it is these
that you'll want to go inside, if at all possible, to experience organizational life. Others, however, are toxic.
You'll want to steer clear of these if you can; they are
afflicted with leaders who obstruct exploration. They

do this because they are blind to the new realities of the knowledge organization.

THE KNOWLEDGE ORGANIZATION

One hundred, fifty, even just twenty-five years ago, the economic landscape was dominated by overweight industrial giants. They got away with being flabby because their competitors were flabby, too. Not only could they afford to be fat; they were *expected* to be. Bloated organizations fulfilled a useful social welfare purpose by providing employment to all. Most jobs were manual and little skilled; workers were expected to leave their brains in the locker room before starting work on the assembly line.

> The real, controlling resource and the absolutely decisive "factor of production" is now neither capital nor land nor labor. It is knowledge. Instead of capitalists and proletarians, the classes of the post-capitalist society are knowledge workers and service workers.
>
> *Peter Drucker*

For better or for worse, those days have gone. Give credit or blame to rapid advances in technology, the lowering of trade barriers, competition from developing, especially Asian, economies, and changing demographics. Organizations today need brains, not brawn.

Microsoft Corporation is often cited as the ultimate knowledge organization. Its tangible assets are negligible, yet its market value is several hundred billion dollars. Where, then, does the value lie? In the brains of its workforce. This is why the *New York Times* said that Microsoft's only factory asset is "the imagination of its workers."

Even in manufacturing companies, the manual workers who physically handle the product are in a minority. They are outnumbered by knowledge workers: managers, designers, marketers, accountants, advertisers, planners, coordinators, and all the rest.

It is not huge factories and sophisticated plants that provide a company with competitive advantage these days, but rather the knowledge of its permanent workforce. Since increasingly the permanent workforce is dominated by knowledge workers, Charles Handy calls it "the professional core." It is comprised of, he writes, "the people who are essential to the organization. Between them they own the organizational knowledge that distinguishes that organization from its counterparts. Lose them and you lose some of yourself."

What is the primary function of those in the professional core? Yes, they do own the company's special knowledge. That, however, is only a secondary function, because one thing is certain: The knowledge that is sufficient today to give the company a competitive advantage will be inadequate tomorrow. The company needs to keep reinventing its knowledge base. It does this by constantly creating new knowledge. It is this that is the primary function of the professional core.

Creativity. Dynamism. Innovation. Risk taking. Openness to change. Flexibility. Continuous learning. Constant reinvention. You will make a grave mistake if you dismiss these as merely the buzzwords of gurus. No matter which organization you work for, it will be the ability of the professional core to display these behaviors that will, more than anything else, determine whether the organization is healthy, sick, or dead in a decade's time.

> Tomorrow's effective "organization" will be conjured up anew each day.
> *Tom Peters*

WHICH WOULD *YOU* CHOOSE TO WORK FOR?

The professional core is typically comprised of well-educated people—nearly all have tertiary qualifications of one kind or another. They are undoubtedly intelligent. But intelligence is a plentiful commodity. If that alone were needed to build a strong professional core, then any firm could acquire it in spades.

Sadly, many firms act as if this *is* all that is needed—they fill themselves up with intelligent people, but wonder why they constantly struggle to survive. Well, here's why.

Assume that you are an explorer and that you have the chance to join one of two competing firms. They are identical, except for the attributes of their respective professional cores.

The professional core of the first—let's call it a "calling organization"—consists mainly of explorers like you. They work for this organization because, although they could work elsewhere, this is where they want to be right now. Accustomed as they are to confronting hard but fundamental questions in their personal lives—*What really matters? What are my values? What are my priorities? Why?*—they bring this same inquiring mind-set to their work, along with all the passion and creative energies that flow to those who are seeking or following their bliss. They are constantly pushing out their own boundaries. As they do so, their ability to create new knowledge for the organization is enhanced.

The professional core of the second—let's call it a "career organization"—is dominated by people whose work is a career, a way of earning a living. They are every bit as intelligent as their counterparts in the calling organization, they are technically as competent, and they work just as hard. But their heart isn't in their work. Most of them suffer from insecurity and other numbing symptoms of angst. They work somewhat mechanistically; not that they are devoid of new ideas, but the true creative spark is missing. They lack passion, for they are not following, or indeed even looking for, their bliss.

Which of these two professional cores is more likely to be effective at its primary task of creating new knowledge for the organization? And which is more likely to provide you with a dynamic, challenging, growth-promoting work environment? The answer is obvious. If you had the chance to join either of these two organizations, you would doubtless opt for the calling organization.

The A's are people who are filled with passion, committed to making things happen, open to ideas from anywhere, and blessed with lots of runway ahead of them. They have the ability to energize not only themselves, but everyone who comes in contact with them.

*Jack Welch
(CEO of GE)*

"The world we have created is a product of our way of thinking," said Einstein. Nothing will change in the future without fundamentally new ways of thinking. This is the real work of leadership.

Peter Senge

"The latest studies seem to show a strong correlation between our troubles and our customers' perceptions that doing business with us is like throwing money down a rathole."

HOW CALLING ORGANIZATIONS ATTRACT PEOPLE LIKE YOU . . .

If you're inside a company, or outside looking in, how can you tell whether it is a calling organization? Here are some clues on what to look for.

First, if it is a calling organization, its professional core will be *full* of explorers—and the leaders will be explorers themselves. Explorers love working with other explorers—people who share their vitality and energy and work values. Conversely, they get frustrated by career types who unwittingly serve as a sea anchor,

> In today's environment, when you boil it all down, the principal enemy is inertia.
>
> *Tom Peters*

holding the firm back by resisting change, tolerating mediocrity, creating bureaucratic barriers, finding problems instead of solutions, dumping negativity into the workplace, and sucking energy out of it.

Second, those within the professional core of a calling organization share a commitment to a set of fundamental values. These values vary, of course, from firm to firm, but generally include integrity, a striving for excellence, a dedication to working cooperatively and sharing know-how, a love of learning, and an ethic of constant improvement. The commitment to these values is not just mouthed; it is real, visceral.

Third, the leaders of a calling organization are willing to entrust people in the professional core with a large measure of autonomy. Most knowledge workers cherish their autonomy, but explorers do so especially. Having been told what result is expected from them, they want to be left alone to achieve that result in their own way. Seek to pin them down too much and they champ at the bit. This grant of substantial autonomy is less risky in a calling organization than in a career organization, for the shared values provide an overriding framework.

Fourth, the leaders of a calling organization have a genuine and deep interest in and concern for people and their development. They respect individual differences. More than that, they cherish diversity, recognizing that diversity feeds creativity.

> [GE is creating] an atmosphere where people dare to try new things— where people feel assured in knowing that only the limits of their creativity and drive, their own standards of personal excellence, will be the ceiling on how far and how fast they move.
>
> *Jack Welch*

. . . AND HOW THEY LET THEM GO

There is one other key clue. If you join a calling organization, its leaders will be dedicated to your personal growth and professional development—so dedicated that they will be willing to support you to move out of and away from the organization when you want to continue your exploring elsewhere.

This is not altruism run amok. Such leaders are acting in their organization's best interests. If they staff the professional core with explorers—and they should—they have to accept the inevitable corollary, which is that good people will come and go. After all, it is in the very nature of explorers that, instead of living static lives, they are constantly growing and moving forward in their lives.

The leaders of a calling organization have considerable scope for influencing the amount of time that you choose to remain there as an employee. The more they allow you opportunities to explore within the organization, the longer you will stay and contribute. Sooner or later, however, you will probably want to move on, and they should not stand in your way.

> It is hard to prevent the brains walking out of the door if they want to. . . . Intelligence is a leaky form of property.
> *Charles Handy*

When, having rendered great service, you leave to explore elsewhere, it is of course a sad event for the calling organization. But it has its positive side, too. For a start, the loyalty of other employees is strengthened because the leaders have demonstrated vividly that their commitment to the well-being of staff is genuine. And such loyalty matters. Leaders don't want to be in the position of having to buy loyalty with a checkbook. Far better to earn it through establishing a constructive relationship whereby staff, because of the way they are treated, choose to stay with the organization.

More than that, if you have been treated decently and with respect, then even after leaving you remain in a sense forever part of the organization, no longer inside it but, like an alumnus, still belonging to its extended community. And so the calling organization creates for itself, out of you and other such people who move on and the organizations that you subsequently join or create, an extended web of talent and information. This web reaches into the world outside. It gives the calling organization access to a rich source of support for its future efforts to create new knowledge.

THE TOXIC ORGANIZATION

The leaders of a career organization, by contrast, take quite a different approach. They fill the professional core with solid, reliable, but passionless career types. They pay lip service to training and development, but don't take too close an interest in staff, and certainly don't unsettle them by encouraging them to explore. They try to hold on to them, even when it's clear that they would be happier someplace else. And when staff jump from the frying pan into someone else's fire, the leaders rail against their disloyalty while replacing them with others equally passionless.

"Dilbert" © 1993 Scott Adams. Reprinted with permission of United Media. All rights reserved.

The gradual decline of the career organization relative to its competitors is assured. No matter how well it may appear to be doing today, it will inevitably be outperformed in creating the new knowledge that will be needed to succeed tomorrow—outperformed by the competitors whose professional core, comprised of explorers, brings true passion to the task of creating new knowledge.

Kurt was the chairman of a career organization. We had been talking about the idea that people should work at what they love. "You're a subversive," he declared.

"Keep well away from my people. If they hear that sort of stuff from you, they'll leave in droves."

He said it, of course, half jokingly. Which means that he said it half seriously. When I suggested to him that his people ought to be hearing "that sort of stuff" from him, not me, he smiled sympathetically and, convinced that I had finally taken leave of my senses, led me to the bar.

Kurt's reaction is all too typical. Too many chairmen and CEOs mouth the platitude that "our people are our greatest asset," yet show by their acts that they don't believe it. If you suggest to them that their top people should be encouraged to explore and grow and, if necessary, leave, then, like Kurt, they may accuse you of subversion.

They are wrong. It is they who are the *true* subversives.

> Wealth comes not to the rulers of slave labor but to the liberators of human creativity, not to the conquerors of land but to the emancipators of mind.
>
> *George Gilder*

THIRTEEN

Flexibility

Things fall apart; the centre cannot hold.

W. B. YEATS

THE FRAGMENTING ROCK FACE . . .

Picture a vertical rock face, a mighty, monolithic slab towering above land or water. At first glance it appears utterly barren, incapable of sustaining life. Then, looking more closely, you notice that here and there a shrub, maybe even a tree, has miraculously found a toehold. You see mosses, grasses, and other miniature plants punctuating the gray starkness of the rock. And then you see the splinters, the cracks, the fractures, the fissures. The slab of rock is succumbing to environmental forces. Inexorably it is fragmenting. And on the fringes of each fragment, a boundless variety of new life takes hold.

. . . AND THE FRAGMENTING WORLD OF WORK

Barring only his years of war service, my father had but one employer during his entire lifetime. He joined a bank when he left school and left it when he retired forty years later. This was a normal pattern in his day. Even had he been tempted to explore, it would have been perilously hard for him to do so in the work environment that then prevailed.

But that environment has changed irrevocably. Organizations have fragmented, and with them the old concepts of lifetime careers and job security. Competitive forces are driving this fragmentation.

Tom Peters and Robert Waterman encapsulated the new imperatives in their management classic, *In Search of Excellence*. "Stick to your knitting," they advised businesses. By which they meant: Decide what it is that you are going to do, do it exceptionally well, and sell off or contract out the rest. Alternatively, suffer a slow and painful death.

"Stick to your knitting" has led companies to focus their resources. They have "downsized," "delayered," and "outsourced." Delayering has involved stripping away layers of middle management to enhance responsiveness. Outsourcing has involved delegating peripheral activities, formerly executed in-house, to other firms that specialize in these activities.

These changes have had dramatic impacts on the workforce. Some, of course, have been tragic. The unskilled, whom yesterday's flabby companies would have accommodated, now find themselves in a despairing pool of long-term unemployed or, if lucky enough to find occasional work, earning less in real terms now than twenty years ago. Then there are those who have skills—but skills, alas, that are in plentiful supply. They too find work hard to come by, especially if aged over fifty.

The impacts, however, have also been positive. Many have discovered that finding work no longer has to mean (as it has traditionally meant for most people) "finding an organization to employ me"; it can now

> The days of the mammoth corporations are coming to an end. People are going to have to create their own lives, their own careers, and their own successes. Some people may go kicking and screaming into the new world, but there is only one message there: You're now in business for yourself.
>
> *Robert Schaen*
> *(Ameritech manager)*

mean "finding clients to engage me." And it no longer has to mean "having a full-time job"; it can now mean "having several jobs" or "mixing spells of paid work with spells of unpaid but still rewarding work." In short, fragmentation has destroyed the old monolithic work environment and created a profusion of options, most of which were simply not available to earlier generations. The result is that the opportunities for exploring, outside as well as inside the organization, are greater than ever before.

THE FIVE MAIN OPTIONS

Nobody has a shrewder eye for the changing patterns of work than Charles Handy. He has described those changes, and peered into the future to predict their implications, in such books as *The Age of Unreason* and *The Elephant and the Flea*.

Yesterday's overweight organization, Handy says, has been on a weight loss and fitness program. In its new incarnation, it is the shamrock organization. Like the plant from which it draws its name, it has three leaves. The first is the professional core, the second the contractual fringe, and the third the flexible labor force. They are, he says, "made up of three very different groups of people, groups with different expectations, managed differently, paid differently, organized differently."

These, then, are the first three options open to you in the new, fragmented environment. The other two options are the personal specialist, who provides services to people in the professional core, and the portfolio worker, whose varied working life includes significant components of unpaid work.

Let's now look at each of these five options in more detail.

> The "job" is a historical phenomenon, and as such it has a limited expectancy.... We have to recognize that the job is not part of God's creation.... Organizations are hiring, paying, and organizing people to get work done in ways that have little to do with "jobs."
>
> *William Bridges*

Option A: The Professional Core

As we saw in the previous chapter, the professional core contains the shamrock organization's permanent workforce. It consists mainly of professionals, technicians, and managers—highly skilled knowledge workers with (usually) tertiary qualifications. They own, and are responsible for renewing, the company's special knowledge: the knowledge that underpins its competitive advantage.

Because those who work in the professional core are indispensable, the company lavishes material rewards on them—high salary, status, car, and other perks. In return, employees in the professional core work punishing hours—fifty, sixty, or even a hundred hours a week. The formula, says Handy, is ½ x 2 x 3—half as many people, getting paid twice as much, and producing three times as much.

What's it like for those in the core? Well, it depends. Matt and Dianne are senior managers in the same firm. Both work sixty-five hours a week; both earn high salaries. But whereas Matt is in a career, Dianne is in her calling. What a fundamental difference this makes. Matt is selling his soul to the firm. Not so Dianne—work nourishes *her* soul. As she put it to me, "I love working here. To receive a high salary as well—that's pure bonus." The two of them have struck quite different deals. Matt's Faustian bargain involves bartering long hours and angst in exchange for money. Dianne, by contrast, is bartering long hours in exchange for money and bliss.

Most graduates embarking on their working lives head first into the professional core. There is nothing wrong with that, as long as they have the explorer's mind-set. The tragedy arises when, like Matt, they become stuck there and fail to see that this is not the only option but rather one among many. If they would only explore, they would find that other options may suit them much better.

> The theory is that the greater a person's wealth, the more freedom he will have to act as he wishes. . . . However, the system usually requires an enormous and prolonged sacrifice of personal freedom—that is, a structured career—before delivering this material independence.
>
> *John Ralston Saul*

From "The Full Alex" published by Headline. Reprinted with permission of Peattie & Taylor.

Option B: The Contractual Fringe

One firm's peripheral activity is another's core activity. So the shamrock organization, instead of doing peripheral work in-house as previously, now contracts it out to the specialists, thereby getting (it assumes) a better job for less. These specialists comprise the shamrock organization's contractual fringe.

The contractual fringe of any shamrock organization is likely to include both firms and individuals. Some of those firms may be gigantic, others small. And they themselves are shamrock organizations, with their own professional cores and their own contractual fringes. As Handy says, it is "a Chinese box type of world."

The individuals in the contractual fringe are typically self-employed consultants. Often, indeed, the consultant is a former employee. Examples abound of an employee being laid off in the course of downsizing, then immediately being engaged as a contractor to do precisely the same work but now for a fee, not a salary.

The working lives of individuals on the contractual fringe vary enormously. They may work for several firms in a day, or just one in six months. They may work mainly at home or mainly at the premises of clients. They may work by themselves or in partnership with others. They may have ample work as long as they nurture a small stable of existing clients, or they may need to market aggressively to win new clients. They have

> The skills you need to develop . . . are less often associated with being a good employee than they are with being a successful small-business operator. . . . You'll be running your career as a business regardless of whether you are an employee for your present employer, an employee for a new employer, or an independent worker who contracts to do projects.
>
> *William Bridges*

probably discovered that their low overheads and freedom from bureaucratic constraints give them extraordinary pricing flexibility, thus easing the task of finding new clients. They can work at charge-out rates half those of their competitors in large professional firms and still earn a good income. And by offering to do the first job for little or no charge, they can often persuade a prospective client to try them out and thereby establish a potentially long-term relationship.

"I'm free!" said Karen gleefully. The marketing director of a bank, she had just resigned to set up a marketing consultancy. It was clear enough in her mind: Liberated from her employment, she could now be picky about whom to work for and what projects to take on. Moreover, she would design a flexible working life around her own lifestyle preferences. It didn't work out that way. A year later, her work hours and her stress levels were higher than ever before. Fundamentally nothing had changed: She was still in a career, not a calling.

Henry, in contrast, quit his finance job with a health insurer to become an information technology consultant, specializing in medical practices. Though he had had little professional involvement in IT, he was a passionate computer buff. He had helped his sister-in-law, an MD, set up her IT systems; she in turn had recommended him to a few of her colleagues. He cultivated his first clients with the passion and dedication of Jerry Maguire. Thanks mainly to word-of-mouth referrals, his business has now snowballed. Like Karen, he is busier than ever before. Unlike her, however, he is in his bliss.

You will repeat Karen's mistake if you assume self-employment and liberation to be one and the same thing. They are not. You can be free or imprisoned inside the professional core of an organization, depending on whether you are following your bliss. And you can be free or imprisoned if self-employed, again depending on whether you are following your bliss.

"I'm pleased to say that I'm unemployable now!" one man said, meaning that he would never want to work inside an organization again.

Charles Handy

Option C: The Flexible Labor Force

The third leaf of the shamrock consists of part-time and temporary workers. Some of them have these roles by necessity; they would like a permanent, full-time job, but lack the skills to get one. Increasingly, however, people place themselves in the flexible labor force by choice.

Ricky, a gifted designer, has been wooed by many firms who would love to have him join their permanent staff. But no blandishments are sufficient to entice him back into the professional core where he once worked. He prefers to alternate between periods of full-time work and periods of no work at all, during which he spends time with his family and indulging his hobbies.

Those who choose the flexible option enter into a classic win-win arrangement with the shamrock organization. It suits them to remain outside the permanent, full-time core. But it also suits the organization to draw on a flexible labor force as and when needed. It saves money by not employing these people during times of low demand. It often saves on physical costs, too, for many of the flexible labor force work from home.

Option D: The Personal Specialist

They're no slouches. The top knowledge workers who serve the shamrock organization, either as members of its professional core or as independent contractors, work *hard*. As Charles Handy has pointed out, someone who left school at age fifteen a few decades ago and worked forty-hour weeks until retirement at age sixty-five would have worked around a hundred thousand hours over the course of fifty years. Nowadays, knowledge workers might clock up those hours in a mere thirty years.

How do they cope with such long hours? With great difficulty, most of them—but that's not the answer I'm looking for. Let me rephrase the question: How do they manage the rest of their lives when work consumes such

> The cost of a thing is the amount of what I will call life which is required to be exchanged for it, immediately or in the long run.
>
> *Henry David Thoreau*

> [Many New York lawyers follow a] grim ritual of all-nighters, tepid take-out dinners, bleary-eyed vigils at printing houses, Dial-a-Cabs, atrophied social lives, and neglected marriages.
>
> *David Margolick*

a vast chunk of their waking hours? The answer is that, like the shamrock organization, they contract out non-core activities.

And how! They engage a financial planner to manage their share portfolio, a computer consultant to configure their home network, a personal trainer to design and enforce a fitness program. They engage an art consultant to buy a painting for their living room, a landscaper to create a picture-book garden, and a caterer to turn out cordon bleu fare when they entertain at home. They engage nannies to mind their preschoolers and dance instructors and tennis coaches to develop the older children during school vacations. They can afford to do all this because they get paid so much. And they choose to do it because life in the professional core leaves them little discretionary time.

The fact is that one of the world's biggest growth industries is the provision of specialized personal services to overworked but affluent knowledge workers. Each day, new niches are spotted; and in those niches new services are created. Here is a profusion of new work opportunities—opportunities that may enable you to pursue your calling without needing to belong to a shamrock organization at all.

> [P]ortfolio living forces us to think in terms of the circle, something like a pie chart with different segments marked off for different occupations, each colored for kind and degree of hoped-for remuneration. Some occupations will be paid in money, some in other kinds of reward: love, creative satisfaction, power, joy, and the like. And of course the chart will be constantly changing.
>
> *Charles Handy*

Option E: The Work Portfolio

What Charles Handy calls "the work portfolio" is a mix-and-match option. Taking a dollop of this and adding a pinch of that, you concoct a rich working life of many components. The mix evolves as you yourself change.

To get the idea, read how Handy describes his own portfolio: "150 days fee work (at varying rates and including provision for administration, paperwork and abortive meetings with clients); 50 days gift work (for various associations, societies, and groups); 75 days study (essential to keep up-to-date in my work); 90 days homework and leisure."

What may strike you first about Handy's portfolio is that it appears to rest on an expanded concept of work, one that goes beyond paid activities. It includes such things as study and leisure, along with "homework," which is comprised not simply of "housework" but of activities like gardening and playing with the children.

This concept of work accords with the dictionary definition: Work is "expenditure of energy, striving, application of effort to some purpose." It is not Handy who has *expanded* the concept of work; it is we who have *confined* it. The work portfolio restores work to its rightful place as an integrating force at the heart of a full, balanced, and healthy life. It is ideal if you wish to conduct a multidimensional working life that reflects the different parts of your being.

It may be, for example, that you love two types of work but are reluctant to sacrifice one for the other; a work portfolio could enable you to pursue both. Or perhaps the particular passion that constitutes your bliss is such that, by its very nature, it will never yield even a modest family income. In the orthodox view, which would place you in full-time employment, that passion would have to be relegated to, at best, an occasional hobby. A portfolio, on the other hand, may permit you to include it as a core component of your working life. All you need to do (perhaps in conjunction with your partner, having worked out what between you must be earned to meet the family's modestly defined needs) is incorporate into your portfolio a component that is avowedly mercenary—a component that you may not enjoy but that does produce dollars. Thereby, your economic needs having been satisfied, you are liberated to devote the balance of your time to pursuing your calling.

On the other hand, the portfolio option won't be right for you if you are uninterested in personal growth and your main aim is to maximize your income. If this is so, then join the professional core of an organization,

> If you really love to be an engineer, or a scientist, or if you can plant a tree, or paint a picture, or write a poem, not to gain recognition but just because you love to do it, then you will find that you never compete with another. I think this is the real key: to love what you do.
>
> *Krishnamurti*

or work full-time as an independent contractor or personal specialist. Sure, these options may involve selling your soul, but you ought to get a good price for it.

If you have a work portfolio, where will your income come from? Here and there. Your clients might include individuals as well as, or instead of, organizations. Sometimes you might work full-time on a project for just one client for a period of weeks or months. At other times you might work for several different clients in the course of a single week. You might be paid a preagreed sum, or a fee based on time spent on the job, or a salary for part-time work. There might be times when your partner brings in the family income, freeing up your time for parenting, study, or developing a new interest. There might be times when you would like to be earning but can't find paid work, and other times when you have too much paid work.

This may sound like a vision of an insecure future. But the only reliable security is sourced within. If your work portfolio gives you the space to explore, to keep learning and growing, to become the person your Core Self wants to be, it will bring you more security than a highly paid but unfulfilling career in the professional core.

> To me the only answer, I gradually realized, was to be my own master and employer. Today I am a self-employed writer and teacher. It is financially more perilous but in every other way more secure. I can't now escape from myself in my work, but these days I don't want to so much. Being and doing are closer.
>
> *Charles Handy*

FLEXIBILITY RULES

With organizations fragmenting, then, new forms of work have proliferated. You could follow the orthodox path and be a full-time employee belonging to the professional core of a company. But alternatively, it is open to you to be an independent contractor; a part-time employee; a temporary employee; a personal specialist; or a portfolio worker. At different stages of your life, all of these could suit you.

Opportunities for exploration abound in the new

flexible environment. Cast off the old static paradigm that says you have to be a full-time employee. Before you lies an expansive menu of options. Grab the chance to lead a fluid working life—one that honors your Core Self, takes you constantly in the direction of your potentialities, and steers you to your calling.

We need to stop looking at work as simply a means of earning a living and start realizing that it is one of the elemental ingredients of making a life.

Luci Swindoll

The Barriers

FOURTEEN

Fear

I'd said to him, "Now, Cassius, tell me the truth. Put aside all the hoopla, all the bravado. What do you think about Sonny Liston?" And he'd started, "Oh, that big ugly bear." I said, "Forget that, and tell me the truth. What's going to happen?" And Cassius got very thoughtful and then he said, "Well, I'm like Columbus. I think the world is round, but I'm a little scared because now I'm reaching the point where I'll find out if it's really round and I can sail around it or is it flat and will I fall off. I think I can beat him. I think I'm going to do what I say. But I won't know for sure until I get there."

MORT SHARNIK (TALKING ABOUT MUHAMMAD ALI)

LIFE IS SCARY

Ghouls have populated the fairy tales and folk legends of all peoples from time immemorial. Goblins and gremlins too, wicked stepmothers, wart-covered ogres, fire-breathing dragons, multiheaded monsters, big bad wolves, terrifying spirits of the underworld.

All these grisly beings are, of course, creations of our own psyche. We create them for one simple reason: Life is scary.

Tens of thousands of years ago, your ancestors sat

From ghoulies and ghosties and long-leggety beasties And things that go bump in the night, Good Lord, deliver us!

The Cornish or West Country Litany

around a fire at night on the African savanna. And they wondered . . . Would the sun goddess on whom they depended for light and warmth return? Would benign spirits favor them with a successful hunt the next day so that the family could be fed? How could they appease the angry spirits tormenting their child so as to free her from fever? The flames cast a comforting circle of light, but predators waited hopefully in the darkness beyond, their presence betrayed by gleaming eyes.

> It's not that I'm afraid to die. I just don't want to be there when it happens.
>
> *Woody Allen*

For your ancestors, life was scary. For you, what is different? Sure, you have new superstitions. Your nakedness in the vast and mysterious universe is better disguised. You may have built around you an apparently impregnable edifice of social, financial, and intellectual defenses. You may even have succeeded in convincing yourself, like Sherman McCoy in *The Bonfire of the Vanities,* that you are the Master of the Universe. Sorry—it's all illusion.

Nature has played a trick on you. It has endowed your species with greater consciousness than any other creature possesses. You can project yourself outward in space and time. You can make informed guesses of what your world was like billions of years ago; you can communicate, though music and poems and stories, with generations as yet unborn; you can survey the heavens with telescopes, and cells with microscopes; you can travel in fantastic flying machines and explore the floor of the oceans.

And yet—and here's the rub—your consciousness also makes you aware: aware of the randomness with which nature visits suffering upon creatures great and small, aware of your own mortality. You know that, sooner or later, you will be back in the ground, food for worms. And you know to expect a fair amount of pain along the way. Life will inevitably deal some cruel cards to you. Maybe you have another five decades to live, maybe another five days. Maybe your children will outlive you, maybe a tragedy will tear them away. Maybe you'll live able-bodied until dying peacefully in your sleep, maybe you'll spend years bedridden. You just don't know. As a graffiti writer put it, "Life's a bitch, and then you die."

And what's the scariest thing of all? It is to face life alone. Nothing is more likely to accentuate your vulnerability, your frailty, your apparent impotence in the face of overwhelming forces, than to be a free individual, living out your private dreams, risking failure and disapproval.

Which is precisely why you should expect to feel scared if you leave the familiar world of convention and make your own path through life.

> And yet I found that I was afraid. I was afraid to step out of my own little tribe, my own little narrow circle. I was afraid to take the risk of stepping into anything unknown. And most importantly, I was afraid that I just couldn't make any difference anyway.
>
> *Joseph Jaworksi*

APPEASING THE GHOULS BY BUILDING A PRISON

One way of coping with the terrors of life and death is to appease the ghouls. This involves shrinking back from life in an attempt to find shelter and protection and safety. How do you do this? You reduce your own freedom. The trouble with freedom is that it makes the responsibility for the way you live your life undeniably yours. This means that if you are too scared to live the life that nature intends you to live, you are confronted squarely with your own lack of courage. So what do you do? You dispose of your freedom and create for yourself a prison whose walls are built of obligation and convention.

> Liberty means responsibility. That is why most men dread it.
>
> *George Bernard Shaw*

This provides several benefits. First, it lets you off the hook. You now have the perfect excuse. By crowding your day-to-day life with things you *have* to do, you leave no room for exploring. With your life so mired in temporal concerns, you cannot reproach yourself for ignoring the call of your Core Self. You can tell yourself reassuringly that you will answer the call at some unspecified future time when your circumstances have changed and your obligations have receded.

Second, it relieves your sense of puniness. No longer are you alone: You belong to, and subscribe to the conventions of, the family, the gang, the club, the team, the organization, the nation. While your own life may be distinctly unheroic, you derive a vicarious sense of heroism from the achievements of the collective.

Third, it provides the illusion of safety in numbers. Convention has you walking down well-trodden paths. You will meet plenty of others along the way. And you can convince yourself that, rather than follow the mysterious, "irrational" promptings of your Core Self, it is safe to go with the crowd.

Fourth, it removes the responsibility for making choices. By adopting a posture of unthinking compliance with social conventions, you will be steered toward "sensible" options that bring you approving applause.

And fifth, it gives you something to rail against. If only your colleagues didn't need you so much, if only your children were older, if only, if only, if only . . . It's great to have a scapegoat to blame for your angst.

THE PRICE OF APPEASEMENT

Embedding yourself in the here and now, filling your life with obligation, allowing the agenda of your life to be set by others—these, then, are the most common strategies undertaken, unconsciously of course, to provide a defense against the ghouls.

Unfortunately, they are about as effective as eating garlic to relieve bad breath. By shrinking back from life, you guarantee that a growing angst will gnaw insidiously away at you. You see, your Core Self won't be fooled. It knows what life you are meant to be living, and it isn't going to forget.

> Ships in harbor are safe, but that's not what ships are built for.
>
> *John Shedd*

> There are persons who shape their lives by the fear of death, and persons who shape their lives by the joy and satisfaction of life. The former live dying; the latter die living.
>
> *Harold Kallen*

Out of fear you may "play it safe" and seek to avoid the risks and dangers inherent in living the full and active life nature intends for you. But by following a conventional path that denies expression to your Core Self, you expose yourself to far greater perils. Angst, as we have seen in chapter 1, comes in various costumes such as insecurity, anxiety, loneliness, boredom, bitterness, isolation, and emptiness. At its root is that gnawing, insidious sense of talents wasted, of life possibilities missed.

The simple fact is that the best way to fuel your fear of death is to fail to live life to the full. Elisabeth Kübler-Ross proffered this advice after a lifetime spent working with the terminally ill: "There is no need to be afraid of death. It is not the end of the physical body that should worry us. Rather, our concern should be to *live* while we're alive—to release our inner selves from the spiritual death that comes with living behind a facade designed to conform to external definitions of who and what we are."

To appease the ghouls, you simply need to give them dominion over your life: Shrink back from the potentialities residing in your Core Self, surrender your freedom, embed yourself in obligations to others, don't explore, don't seek your calling. Do that, and the ghouls will be happy. The more your angst grows—and it will—the happier they will be.

> Live all you can; it's a mistake not to. It doesn't matter what you do in particular, so long as you have had your life. If you haven't had that, what have you had?
>
> *Henry James*

CONFRONTING THE GHOULS

There is an alternative to appeasement. It is to confront the ghouls. Instead of shrinking from life, you embrace it, and all its pleasures and pains, enthusiastically. You do this by exploring, by going to where your Core Self calls you. This and this alone reduces the ghouls' power. But it takes time: The ghouls don't give up easily. Taming them takes not days or weeks but years, sometimes decades.

THE WAY OF THE HERO

Confronting the ghouls is the way of the hero. Some have the idea that heroes are fearless, mysteriously but fortuitously immune from ghouls. Not so. Just like anyone else, they experience fear and self-doubt. Where they differ from nonheroes is that they push on regardless.

Heroes are determined to be true to themselves. By exploring, they keep pushing out the boundaries of their sense of self. When, in the course of expanding their horizons, they come to the point where convention would have them stop, they keep pressing onward, into uncharted territory if necessary.

Humankind has countless tales of heroes, mythical and real. These contain many lessons for you if you wish to vanquish the ghouls. First, you must participate in life. As American psychotherapist Carl Rogers put it, "Launch yourself fully into the stream of life." That is the only way to discover who you really are and why you are here. That is the only way you can convert your possibilities into actualities.

Second, choices need to be made, and *you* need to make them. In Richard Wilbur's poem "Parable," Don

> I went to the woods because I wanted to live deliberately, to front only the essential facts of life, and see if I could not learn what it had to teach, and not, when I came to die, discover that I had not lived.
>
> *Henry David Thoreau*

Quixote has the chance to determine which way he should head on his quest for glory. Arriving at a crossroads, he leaves the decision to his horse. Unfortunately, it chooses to head for the barn. If you fudge your choices or hope that events will make them for you, you too may end up in the barn.

Third, you must expect pain. No pathway through life will insulate you against suffering. The issue is not the avoidance of suffering, for that is impossible. Rather, it is the attitude you bring to suffering. Will you let it defeat you, or will you learn from it and become strengthened by it?

Fourth, you must expect to be scared. By favoring some options and cutting off others, by letting go of the familiar in order to try the new, you will be taking risks. Your fear is a normal and natural response to those risks. Being scared doesn't make you a coward. You're a coward only if you let your fears turn you away from the path that is right for you.

> In some way one must play with life and consent daily to die, to give oneself up to the risks and dangers of the world, allow oneself to be engulfed and used up. Otherwise one ends up as though dead in trying to avoid life and death.
>
> *Ernest Becker*

Do You Want to Live Dying or Die Living?

The ghouls will tell you that, whatever you are, you're no hero. Just take the safe option, they will say. Stick with convention and leave the heroics to others.

It's a seductive message. Yes, instead of exploring, you could stay "safely" at home and let the ghouls imprison you there. But remember that the ghouls are leaving unstated the crippling price of appeasement. That price far outweighs the risks of pushing onward to find your calling. Your angst will grow, your fear of life will grow, your fear of death will grow.

So confront your fears and set off in search of your calling. Do so for the sake of your own well-being. That way, by the time you die, you will have lived. Better by far to die living than to live dying.

> The worst thing that happens in life is not death. The worst thing would be to miss it. A friend of mine . . . says all spiritual paths have four steps: show up, pay attention, tell the truth, and don't be attached to the results. I think the great danger in life is not showing up.
>
> *Dr. Rachel Naomi Remen*

FIFTEEN

Insecurity

At the moment of my greatest despair, from my uncon-
scious there came a sequence of words, like a strange dis-
embodied oracle from a voice that was not mine: "The
only real security in life lies in relishing life's insecurity."
Even if it meant being crazy and out of step with all that
seemed holy, I had decided to be me.

M. SCOTT PECK

THE IMPOSTOR SYNDROME

Marguerite is an extraordinarily good financial analyst. Her
clients think she's great, her colleagues think she's great. And
you could be forgiven for believing that she thinks she's
great, for she maintains an impressive facade of assuredness.

Marguerite's drive, however, is fueled by crippling
insecurity. Privately, she feels like an impostor. "I'm not
what they all think I am," she confessed to me once.
"They think I'm good at what I do, but I'm not. I'm a
fraud. It's just a matter of time before they see that."

She is certainly not alone in feeling this. Insecurity—
feeling inadequate, unworthy, undeserving, unloved, and
unlovable—is one of the most common forms of angst.
Time and again it manifests itself in the impostor syndrome: the nonsensical belief, held by people who excel
in their careers, that they are in fact not up to the mark.

[People] measure their
esteem of each other by
what each other has, and
not by what each is. . . .
Nothing can bring you
peace but yourself.

Ralph Waldo Emerson

Insecure people, naturally enough, try hard to relieve their insecurity. In searching for security, they often see their careers—in particular, a relentless striving to advance up the career ladder—as the answer. In fact, their careers are the problem. For such people, clinging to their careers to relieve insecurity is akin to drinking salt water to relieve thirst.

"Yes, I understand," Marguerite said to me. "I need to break away from this career. I need to explore. And I *will* do so. But I won't do it just yet, because I'm too insecure. Let me fix my self-esteem first. *Then* I'll have the confidence to make the break."

Marguerite *didn't* understand. She was putting the cart before the horse. Security, self-confidence, self-esteem—these weren't things she could acquire before exploring. They were things that would come to her only as a result of exploring.

> We may think there is a sure road. But that would be the road of death. Then nothing happens any longer—at any rate, not the right things. Anyone who takes the sure road is as good as dead.
>
> *Carl Jung*

How *Not* to Find Security

The surest way of fueling your insecurity is to pursue security as an end in itself. Here are three popular pursuit strategies, guaranteed to be 100 percent ineffective.

Pursue Financial Security

The first strategy is to equate your personal insecurity with financial insecurity. This is convenient because it spares you from having to face up to the true source of your insecurity. Instead, it gives you license to focus your attention on a scapegoat: your bank balance.

Financial insecurity takes many forms, but two stand out. The first is a feeling that you need to earn more money. If you can convince yourself that you are insecure because you don't have enough money, it is a small step to convince yourself also that all will be well if you can just build a kind of financial Maginot Line. Achieving a raise, upon a salary review or a promotion or a job change, becomes the goal. It provides a wonderfully tangible focus for your angst.

The nicest thing about this approach is that it can be used whatever your finances. Whether your income is forty thousand dollars or four hundred thousand dollars, whether your net assets are fifty thousand dollars or five million, you can convince yourself that the problem is money simply by taking an ever more expansive view of your "needs." And if you want further persuasion, you can always focus on friends or colleagues who are financially better off than you, letting the "unfairness" of this rankle.

A second form of financial insecurity focuses not on the level of your income, but on its dependability. If you regard with dread the possibility of being out of a job, convince yourself that you will be secure if you can find, or remain in, a job that is unlikely to be threatened by layoffs or dismissal. Accept the likely price of such job security: a stolid career that starves the soul.

Pursue Social Acclaim

The second wonderfully ineffective way to pursue security is to attribute your insecurity to a lack of social status. This involves adopting or staying in a career not

> I believed that money and possessions insulated me from the threats of the outside world. But in insulating myself, I was all the more alone, and the more alone I was, the more vulnerable I felt.
>
> *Dennis Augustine*

Now, don't you think human beings are like that? They dig a little pool for themselves away from the swift current of life, and in that little pool they stagnate, die; and this stagnation, decay, we call existence.

Krishnamurti

because it has anything to do with your calling, but because it is prestigious or will permit you to acquire a splendid house, expensive cars, and other such trappings for public display. This strategy is seductively rational: "I feel like a nobody; I will pursue a career that will attract kudos; the kudos will be proof that I'm not a nobody; ergo I will be secure."

This second strategy, like the first, has the virtue of being universally available. If you're an insecure salesman, you can convince yourself that a promotion to sales manager would cure everything. If you're an insecure lawyer, you need only be made a partner. If you're an insecure CEO, you need only be headhunted to run an even larger company. If you're an insecure king, you need only be appointed God.

Become a Self-Esteem Book Junkie

The third surefire strategy is to read endless "how to improve your self-esteem" books. (Ideally, attend lots of seminars and workshops as well.) The trick here is to read the books, understand intellectually what they are saying, commend them to others, but not—repeat *not*—act upon the advice they proffer. If you are a true junkie, you will never make that mistake. You will read everything that is going on the subject, acquiring thereby both a sense of virtue and an impressive library. But you will never *act* to change the way you live your life.

HOW TO LET SECURITY FIND YOU

Playing it safe is the riskiest choice we can ever make.

Sarah Ban Breathnach

These strategies for pursuing security are not merely ineffective, they are downright dangerous. They require you to treat your Core Self with contempt. They lull you into settling for the stolid security that comes from living a life scripted for you by others. They imprison you in a career that sucks out your vitality, so that your sense of self further erodes and your insecurity gnaws at you ever more remorselessly.

If you are tempted to deal with your own insecurity by pursuing one of these strategies, ask yourself these questions: Why do so many wealthy and acclaimed people suffer from an insecurity so gigantic that it dwarfs yours? And why do so many people with neither wealth nor acclaim have an unshakable security?

The answer to both questions is, of course, the same. Security is not a product of wealth or acclaim. It is sourced from within. It is a by-product. It results from knowing who you are, being centered, living the life that you were born to live, following your calling. And these in turn result from exploring and experimenting, experiencing life, confronting the ghouls by undertaking the hero's life-giving quest of self-discovery.

Security, in short, is like a butterfly. Reach out for it, and it will elude your grasp. Turn away and get on with your life, and it may land uninvited on your shoulder.

> The more inwardly defined you are, the less you need. The less you need, the more power you have.
>
> *Dean Ornish*

IN SEARCH OF SECURITY

In their book *In Search of Excellence,* published in 1982, Tom Peters and Robert Waterman reminded the business world of a simple but neglected truth. Do not pursue profit as an end in itself, they said. Profit is a by-product. It results from attending to your customers and your employees.

For more than two decades now, managers have taken this philosophy to heart. Their organizations are the stronger for it. Yet as individuals many of those same managers suffer from chronic insecurity.

What they should do is paraphrase Peters and Waterman: "Do not pursue security as an end in itself. Security is a by-product. It results from attending to your heart and soul."

> Security is mostly a superstition. It does not exist in nature, nor do the children of humans as a whole experience it. Avoiding danger is no safer in the long run than outright exposure. Life is either a daring adventure or nothing.
>
> *Helen Keller*

SIXTEEN

Disapproval

It is not the critic who counts, not the one who points out how the strong man stumbled or how the doer of deeds might have done them better. The credit belongs to the man who is actually in the arena; whose face is marred with sweat and blood and dust; who strives valiantly; who errs and comes short again and again; who knows the great enthusiasms, the great devotions and spends himself in a worthy cause and who, if he fails, at least fails while daring greatly so that his place shall never be with those cold and timid souls who know neither victory nor defeat.

THEODORE ROOSEVELT

BEING DIFFERENT

It isn't the done thing to eschew the career path. It isn't the done thing to be true to your Core Self. It isn't the done thing to follow your idiosyncratic bliss. It isn't the done thing to find and dedicate your life to your calling.

The crowd (by which I mean adherents to the reigning orthodoxy in any group) doesn't generally take kindly to people who are different. By definition, the crowd is made up of conformists—people who "play the game," fit in, do things in the usual way; people

147

who, by the norms of the group, are sensible, reasonable, responsible, dutiful. They dislike, sometimes even revile, nonconformists.

Which is why nonconformists have had a hard time of it over the centuries. They've been excluded, expelled, excommunicated, excoriated, exiled, exposed, and extirpated. And that's just the lucky ones. Those less fortunate have been crucified, burned at the stake, and stoned. (Some, I grant you, have been exalted. But often that came about only after they had suffered years or decades of less pleasant treatment.)

In short, if you're contemplating following your bliss, you have good cause to be worried that others will disapprove.

CRIME AND PUNISHMENT

George Bernard Shaw once made reference to "a man of great common sense and good taste, meaning thereby a man without originality and moral courage." Conformists—people of "great common sense and good taste"—feel threatened by nonconformists. They find it unsettling to be reminded of their own lack of "originality and moral courage." And so they push nonconformists away to the periphery. They marginalize them, using a variety of techniques.

This hurts. *Homo sapiens* is a social species whose members value, indeed yearn for, a sense of belonging. To feel different or misunderstood is often painful; to feel excluded is even more so. Nobody is immune from this hurt. It is always tempting to think of great figures in heroic terms, imagining them to be indifferent to ostracism, impervious to criticism or ridicule, not caring about the reactions of others as they march boldly into history. The reality, as the examples below show, is far more complex.

When she told her French friends about it, they were amazed. "You mean you don't want to fight the occupation of your country?" She would have liked to tell them that behind Communism and Fascism, behind all occupations and invasions lurks a more basic, pervasive evil and that the image of that evil was a parade of people marching by with raised fists and shouting identical syllables in unison. But she knew she would never be able to make them understand. Embarrassed, she changed the subject.

Milan Kundera

Ostracism

As a nineteen-year-old, Mahatma Gandhi decided to travel to England to study law. His community didn't approve. The headman admonished him: "In the opinion of the caste, your proposal to go to England is not proper. Our religion forbids voyages abroad. We have also heard that it is not possible to go there without compromising our religion. One is obliged to eat and drink with Europeans." Gandhi vowed to adhere to Hindu practices while in England; this failed to assuage the community's anger. In the end, they excommunicated him. "This boy," the headman declared, "shall be treated as an outcast from today. Whoever helps him or goes to see him off at the dock shall be punishable with a fine of one rupee four annas."

> I kept denying my destiny because of my insecurity, my dread of ostracism, my anxiety, and my lack of courage to risk myself.
>
> *Joseph Jaworski*

Criticism

Beethoven revered Haydn, his mentor and teacher. But Haydn personified Europe's musical establishment in the early nineteenth century. He was upset when his protégé began to explore radical new styles. His critical reaction brought about in Beethoven what a mutual friend rather gently called a "sort of apprehension, because he was aware that he had struck out a path for himself which Haydn did not approve of." In truth, Beethoven was deeply hurt, and his close personal relationship with Haydn withered.

> The wisest men follow their own direction And listen to no prophet guiding them.
>
> *Euripides*

Withholding of Deserved Support

Nigel Kennedy doesn't fit the mold of a classical violinist: He is English and, moreover, punkish. As a youth he failed to receive the support his prodigious talents warranted. There was, he later wrote, "an attitude in the profession that as I wasn't Israeli or Russian, I wasn't to be taken seriously."

Incomprehension

Paul Cézanne's departure from artistic norms alienated him even from the art fraternity. "For years, almost until his death," wrote a biographer, "he met with blind incomprehension from the public, dealers and critics; even his friends doubted whether he had the makings of a real artist." Hurt by this disapproval, he adopted an isolated and aloof lifestyle.

> The man who follows the path will usually get no further than the crowd. The man who walks alone is likely to find himself in places no one has ever seen.
>
> *Alan Ashley-Pitt*

Hostility

For many months Pablo Picasso worked on *Les Demoiselles d'Avignon,* a radical painting that has come to be regarded as one of the masterpieces of the twentieth century. When it was nearing completion, he finally showed it to friends. They were appalled. The painting defied not just the classical rules, but also those of the artistic avant garde. As one biographer wrote: "Even his most devoted admirers, Max Jacob and Guillaume Apollinaire, found nothing to praise. . . . Matisse thought the painting a deliberate mockery of the modern movement in art, and vowed he would 'sink' Picasso."

Ridicule

Upon seeing *Les Demoiselles d'Avignon,* Picasso's friend Leo Stein scoffed: "You've been trying to paint the fourth dimension. How amusing!" Sigmund Freud was mocked, too, when in 1896 he gave a lecture to a medical audience in Vienna on his new theory that precocious sexual experiences underpinned hysteria. He received what he described as "an icy reception from the asses." The person presiding at the meeting dismissed Freud's theory as "a scientific fairy tale." The whole experience made Freud so despondent that he gave just one more public medical lecture in Vienna during the remaining forty-two years of his life.

CELEBRATING DIFFERENTNESS

> Let me listen to me, and not to them.
>
> *Gertrude Stein*

And you? If *you* leave the broad paths trodden by the crowd and seek to cut out a path for yourself, you are

Arthur didn't always find it easy to follow his bliss while meeting his father's expectations.

likely to be spared crucifixion, burning, or stoning. But don't expect everyone to applaud you. You too may encounter painful disapproval, perhaps even from family and friends.

Occasionally you may find yourself wishing that you were just one of the crowd. At such times the path of least resistance—the conformist's path—can appear so much easier to traverse than the lonely path into the unknown that you are cutting for yourself.

But always remember: Conformists pay a price. Conformity requires subjugation of your Core Self, denial of what is unique and special in you. The result?—for you, angst, and for society, lost opportunity.

My freedom will be so much greater and more meaningful, the more narrowly I limit my field of action and the more I surround myself with obstacles. Whatever diminishes constraints, diminishes strength. The more constraints one imposes, the more one frees one's self of the chains that shackle the spirit.

Igor Stravinsky

So instead of being put off by disapproval, you need to be spurred on. In *Creating Minds*, Howard Gardner writes about seven of the twentieth century's great nonconformists: Albert Einstein, Sigmund Freud, Pablo Picasso, Igor Stavinsky, T. S. Eliot, Mahatma Gandhi, and Martha Graham. He notes that each of them "used his or her marginality as a leverage in work. Not only did they exploit their marginality in what they worked on and how they worked on it; more important, whenever they risked becoming members of 'the establishment,' they would shift course to attain at least intellectual marginality." He concludes that each "was determinedly marginal and was willing to give up much to retain this marginality."

In effect, marginality amounts to passing a test. It indicates that you are still evolving, still growing, asserting your individuality, taking risks, pushing out your boundaries, realizing your potentialities. Being in the mainstream—being a conformist in the crowd—is evidence of just the opposite.

So what you need to do to sustain yourself is to look upon your differentness as a source of strength, not of weakness. It is something to be celebrated. Remember Carl Jung's words: "Nature is aristocratic, and one person of value outweighs ten lesser ones." Human progress relies on aristocrats: individuals with the moral courage to make their own way, find their own truths, and, in the process, enrich their communities. If the price of being an aristocrat is that you belong on the fringes of the crowd, then so be it. Be different, and be proud of it!

If a man does not keep pace with his companions, perhaps it is because he hears a different drummer. Let him step to the music that he hears, however measured or far away.

Henry David Thoreau

SEVENTEEN

Dishonesty

Sincerity is the key. If you can fake that,
you've got it made.

GROUCHO MARX

BEING A COMPULSIVE LIAR

Liar!

No, don't turn away. It's you I'm addressing. You're the liar.

To whom do you lie? To yourself, of course. You do it all the time. (You're not alone. We all deceive ourselves. Illusion shields us from unpalatable truths.)

The trouble starts when you lie to yourself about truths that you should enthusiastically embrace: truths about the real you, the you residing in your Core Self that yearns for self-expression. You are probably not even aware that you're doing this. If you live a lie long enough, it can seem to be the truth. The fears that prompted the lie in the first place are working all the time to sustain it, to deceive you into believing that you are someone other than the person you really are.

> We are what we pretend to be.
>
> *Kurt Vonnegut, Jr.*

Why does it matter? Because you explore to learn. You explore to gain insights into your Core Self so that, by realigning your working life, you may escape angst and find bliss. Exploring demands honesty from you. Above all, it requires that you stop kidding yourself about your angst.

I'M YOUR ANGST, AND I'M HERE TO HELP YOU

Carl Jung was fond of saying of a patient, "Thank God he became neurotic!" Why? Because the patient had been reluctant to see that he was living a false life and betraying his Core Self. The neurosis had made this falsity manifest. It had forced him to look inward, thus creating the opportunity to put things right. That is why Jung celebrated it.

Your angst, too, is a bearer of truth. It brings a message from your Core Self. The message says, "Whoa! This isn't the life you're meant to be living. You're suffocating me. It's time to change course." This is what your angst means, and if you are honest enough to understand it in this way, you should welcome it.

Unfortunately, the temptation to deceive yourself is immense. The mysterious message from your Core Self is scary. It promises to lure you away from your safe, familiar life and lead you to who knows where. It asks you to defy convention and risk the wrath or derision of the crowd. It calls on you to tear down your veneer of respectability and achievement, and if you do that, you might reveal an ogre within. It threatens, in short, to overturn your world.

And so you kid yourself. Your self-deception takes three main forms.

> All symptoms are honorable. They redirect you. Move forward. The past is over.
>
> *Bernie Siegel*

Kidding Yourself That All Is Well

Problem? What problem? The human capacity for denial, even when evidence of mayhem and misery abounds, is extraordinary.

Are you unsure whether you are in a state of denial? Try standing naked in front of a mirror. Look at the person in the glass coldly, ruthlessly. Imagine you are an inquisitor charged with assessing, by appearance alone, the health (mental, emotional, and spiritual as well as physical) of that person. What do you see? Look at the eyes—are they dull or do they sparkle? Look at the muscles around the mouth, the neck, the shoulders—are they taut or relaxed? Look at the face and complexion—do they reveal a person who is agitated or at peace, stale or vital, stagnant or growing? Look at the posture—is it that of a person who is unsure and off balance, or of someone who is solidly grounded and centered? The signs are there if you are willing to be brutally honest with yourself.

Go for a walk, alone, in a wilderness area—along a beach, through a forest, up to the hilltops, beside a dancing stream as it winds down a valley. Deploy all your senses to tune in to the unvarnished, natural, beautiful reality around you. Hear the birds in the rustling leaves. See the surging, pulsing, foaming waves, and sense the teeming life within them. Smell the rain on the damp earth. Feel the breeze upon your skin. Taste the nectar from the flowers. Then switch your attention to what is going on inside you, and you may find yourself receiving a message from your Core Self that points, in grim contrast to the truth and beauty that surround you, to the falseness of your own life.

Kidding Yourself That the Symptoms Are the Problem

Even if you do acknowledge that there is a problem, you can deceive yourself into believing that it is the

> Denial is not a river in Egypt.
> *Anonymous*

> The ways in which we need to grow are usually those we are the most supremely defended against and are least willing to admit even exist, let alone take an undefended, mindful peek at and then act on to change.
> *Jon Kabat-Zinn*

symptoms that constitute the problem. Instead of recognizing the falseness of your life and seeking to redress it, you attempt the impossible task of eliminating the symptoms. You read books on relieving stress, you trot off to endless courses on stress management (or time management, or self-esteem, or becoming wealthy or happy, and on and on), you take sleeping tablets or Prozac. Such steps often provide temporary relief; for a few days or weeks you may exalt in the feeling that you've cracked the problem. But alas, the symptoms always return in the end because the underlying malaise—the betrayal of your Core Self, the gulf between your work and your calling—remains untreated.

Kidding Yourself That a Scapegoat Is to Blame

Another diversionary technique is to conduct a futile search for scapegoats. All will be well, you decide, if you can change just one thing in your life: get promoted, move to a new division, change your boss, change your firm, change your spouse, change your house. You make the change because it offers the promise of a quick fix and spares you from having to look inward for your failure to answer the call of your Core Self. Again the change may afford temporary relief, but sooner or later the angst returns. When it does, you feel more desperate than ever because you can no longer cling to the hope that this one change will fix everything.

Denying the problem, treating the symptoms, searching for scapegoats—if you fall for these tricks, the progress you make on your journey of exploration will be slow indeed. That is why you need to commit to brutal honesty.

> The ordinary mind has a false, dull stability, a smug and self-protective inertia, a stonelike calm of ingrained habits. [It] is as cunning as a crooked politician, skeptical, distrustful, expert at trickery and guile, "ingenious . . . in the games of deception."
>
> *Sogyal Rinpoche*

GETTING REAL

Like all of us, you will have constructed an impressive array of facades. With these you seek to deceive not only the outside world but also yourself about who you really are.

A popular facade relates to the behaviors of the in-group you want to belong to or impress. Do you affect their mannerisms? Do you adopt their hobbies? Do you read their journals and propound their views? Instead of being yourself, have you become one of them instead?

Another popular facade relates to material success. Do you strive to keep up with—better still, surpass—the Joneses? Do you surround yourself with conspicuous trappings of success, even if you can't really afford them? Do you live in public splendor, although behind closed doors your life is one of private squalor (not materially, but in the desolation of your angst-ridden life)?

To get real, you need to demolish those facades. The longer they have been in place, the scarier and harder this is. Facades erected over decades may take years to pull down. You may feel that an ogre lurks behind them—that if you reveal too much of yourself, others will see a contemptible and ugly creature, one that is beyond love and respect. The truth, of course, is that the only ogre lurking inside is an illusory creation of your own psyche.

> Before I built a wall I'd
> ask to know
> What I was walling in or
> walling out.
>
> *Robert Frost*

From "The Full Alex" published by Headline. Reprinted with permission of Peattie & Taylor.

ONCE MORE—EXPLORE

In the final analysis, there is only one way to strip through the veil of lies, only one way to pull down the facades. That is to intensify your exploring. Indeed, that

What must you give up? All that is not truly you; all that you have chosen without choosing and value without evaluating, accepting because of someone else's extrinsic judgment. . . . What will you gain? Only your own, true self.

Elisabeth Kübler-Ross

is the very point of exploring. If you choose not to explore, or if you simply go through the motions, you embrace falsehood. And who is deceived? Others probably see through your lies. In the end, the only one who is fooled is you.

So don't imprison yourself with your lies any longer. Search out the truth, for it will set you free.

EIGHTEEN

Noise

Do you have the patience to wait till your
mud settles and the water is clear?

Lao-Tzu

HEARING THE STILL QUIET VOICE

Here's a simple test. All you have to do is this: Concentrate on your breathing for ten consecutive breaths. Don't let your mind wander. Think of nothing else for just ten breaths. That's all.

I bet you fail. It's hard, very hard. Your mind *hates* being still. It likes to flit here and there, thinking about yesterday, thinking about tomorrow, thinking about anything but the here and now.

And God knows there is no shortage of things for it to think about. Like the project deadline, and the overdue library books, and your son's birthday, and the war against terrorism, and last night's *Seinfeld* rerun, and the way your colleague shafted you, and the dirty laundry, and why your spouse is grumpy, and the worn tires, and how nice it would be to have a different boss, and

> Our mind is a magazine with a new edition every four seconds.
>
> *Marshall McLuhan*

tonight's big game, and the blocked toilet, and the raise that's overdue, and your daughter's pierced tongue, and the coming vacation, and the contest on the cereal box. Your mind can flit through all that in just a few seconds and still be hungry for more.

Timothy Ward, who tried to learn meditation in a Thai monastery, compares the mind to a radio. Not just any old radio, but one whose tuning dial is in the hands of a monkey. He "cranks it around and around, twiddling from frequency to frequency. The radio plays a jumble of disconnected noises, part of a word, then static, a note of a song. This is the normal state of human awareness. The listening consciousness screens out most of this jumble, selecting fragments here and there across the band."

So what? Does it matter? Sure it matters. Because it stops you hearing.

You see, your Core Self knows. It knows where you are right now. It knows where your organism wants to go. It knows where you will find bliss. And it's telling you all the time. It's telling you right now. But can you hear it? No. Because there's just too much jangle, too much confusion, too much noise.

Somehow you need to turn down the noise. Somehow you need to bring the mind to rest, bring it home. Somehow you need to learn to just be here now. Then and only then will you have a chance of hearing the still quiet voice of your Core Self.

> With an unquiet mind, neither exercise, nor diet, nor physick can be of much use.
>
> *Samuel Johnson*

THE PROFESSOR AND THE KID

Meet Dr. Richard Alpert, former professor of psychology at Harvard, 1960s folk hero (along with colleague Timothy Leary), spokesman for the psychedelic movement, expert on expanded consciousness. Some look up to him as a man who knows Truth.

Yet here he is, stumbling around India, deep in despair, looking for answers. And now, at last, he has found someone who does, truly, seem to know Truth. Someone whom swamis, lamas, holy men of all kinds, welcome as a brother. Someone whom he wants to follow as a disciple. And who is this other guy? He wears a dhoti like Gandhi. He has long blond hair and a beard. He is six feet tall. He's only twenty-three years old. And he's Californian!

How absurd, thinks Alpert. *Who's writing this bizarre script? Here I am—I've come half-way around the world and I'm going to follow, through India, a 23-year-old guy from Laguna Beach, California.*

So the ex–Harvard professor follows this kid all around India. The kid is the guru; the professor is the doting acolyte.

The professor complains of dysentery. And the kid just says, "Well, fast for a few days."

The professor, sitting in meditation, complains of sore hips. And the kid says, "Emotions are like waves. Watch them disappear in the distance on the vast calm ocean."

The professor says, "Did I ever tell you about the time that Tim and I . . ." The kid interrupts. "Don't think about the past. Just be here now."

After a period of silence, the professor says, "How long do you think we're going to be on this trip?" The reply comes: "Don't think about the future. Just be here now."

> There are times when in order to keep ourselves in existence at all we simply have to sit back for a while and do nothing. And for a man who has let himself be drawn completely out of himself by his activity, nothing is more difficult than to sit still and rest, doing nothing at all.
>
> *Thomas Merton*

In eternity there is indeed something true and sublime. But all these times and places are now and here. God himself culminates in the present moment, and will never be more divine in the lapse of all the ages.

Henry David Thoreau

As Alpert (now the well-known spiritual teacher Ram Dass) wrote later, "He had just sort of wiped out my whole game. That was it—that was my whole trip— emotions, and past experiences, and future plans."

The kid practiced what he preached; he concentrated on "being here now," all the time. Alpert was moved to write about him, "I never felt so profound an intimacy with another human being."

That's the power that comes from turning down the noise.

SHUTTING UP THE MONKEY

How then are you to shut up the dial-twiddling monkey, or at least get it to turn down the volume? One thing is required for sure. You need to create spaces in your life—spaces for silent time alone, time for just *being*. Ideally there should be at least one such space in your life every day.

One of the best uses to which you can put your silent time alone is to practice some form of meditation or yoga. These disciplines awaken you to what is going on within—the clenching of the jaw, the tightness in the shoulders, the knot in the stomach; thoughts, fears, hopes; your feelings of pain, happiness, weakness, strength, guilt, boredom, ecstasy, or whatever else may be flowing through your being from moment to moment. And they help you tune in to your intuition— those gut feelings whose wisdom your "rational" mind so often shuts out. They help you, in short, to be here now, and thus to hear your Core Self.

Meditation is a word that intimidates many people. They think it involves something strange and mystical. Or they get hung up on having the "best" technique. But it's not about technique: It's simply about experiencing silence by spending quiet, aware, contemplative time alone.

If you feel you need some guidance, try one of these masterly books: Jon Kabat-Zinn's *Wherever You Go, There You Are,* Jack Kornfield's *A Path with Heart,* and Thich Nhat Hanh's *Peace Is Every Step.* Alternatively, take up yoga classes.

Meditation and yoga both demand great discipline. To get the full benefit, you need to incorporate them into your daily routine and persevere with them. If you feel unable or unready to make such a commitment, then at least take time to relax. Take the vacations that are due to you. (You would be astonished at how many angst sufferers fail to do this.) Build pure relaxation time into the weekends. And try to insert short periods of relaxing solitude into your daily life as often as possible. Just sitting in a park or garden, for example, and focusing on what is before and around you—the shades, the shapes, the textures, the aromas, the play of light, the birdsong—can quiet your monkey mind and enliven your sensitivity so that you begin to tune in to the still quiet voice of your Core Self.

> You must have a room, or a certain hour or so a day, where you don't know what was in the newspapers that morning, you don't know who your friends are, you don't what you owe anybody, you don't know what anybody owes to you. This is a place where you can simply experience and bring forth what you are and what you might be
>
> *Joseph Campbell*

ENERGIZING THE MONKEY

Practices like meditation, yoga, and relaxation help calm the monkey. But many commonplace practices of modern life do exactly the opposite. Two stand out.

The first is a bad diet. Certain fats, refined sugar, stimulants (caffeine taken by drinking tea or coffee, nicotine taken by smoking, cocaine, amphetamines), alcohol—all inject toxins into your system or contribute to their buildup, rendering the monkey more agitated than ever.

The second is inadequate exercise. Again, it's astonishing how many angst sufferers are in lousy physical shape. The whole mind-body system then suffers, and if that's out of kilter, it's more power to the monkey.

If you want to learn more about healthy diets and healthy exercise, I suggest you read *Dr. Dean Ornish's*

> The best doctors in the world are Doctor Diet, Doctor Quiet, and Doctor Merryman.
>
> *Jonathan Swift*

Program for Reversing Heart Disease. Its title belies its real scope. What it does is describe the elements of healthy living, with special reference to the three keystones touched on in this chapter: meditation, diet, and exercise.

The Thirsty Fish

In Janwillem van de Wetering's book *The Empty Mirror,* the tale is told of a Japanese teenager, the spoiled only son of two doctors, who was orphaned when both his parents were killed in a car accident. Lost, alienated, rebellious, bitter, angry, adrift in the world but wanting to understand the meaning of his parents' death, he turned for guidance to a Zen master.

"I won't tell you anything," the master said. "You know the answer yourself."

The boy understood this to mean that he should become a monk and meditate to uncover the answers he sought. "Why should I do that?" he asked. "I am rich, I own a large house. I am intelligent, I can go to the university and become a doctor as my parents did. I can have girlfriends and have children and my children will be well off, too. Why should I give it all up to find out something which, you say, I already know?"

"Well, don't then," replied the master. "I never told you to become a monk. You can do what you like."

"If I do become a monk," asked the boy, "will you then help me reach the point that you say I have already reached?"

"I suppose I'll have to," the master said. "But you are like a fish saying it is thirsty."

Are you a thirsty fish, craving answers that are right there, inside you already? If you will only quell the noise generated by your angst, you will hear those answers. Listen to your Core Self, for it is pointing the way forward to your calling.

Joseph Campbell: He is the one that evokes compassion, the poor chap. To see him stumbling around when all the waters of life are right there really evokes one's pity.

Bill Moyers: The waters of eternal life are right there? Where?

Joseph Campbell: Wherever you are—if you are following your bliss, you are enjoying that refreshment, that life within you, all the time.

NINETEEN

Impatience, Indiscipline, Indolence

If a thing is worth doing, it is worth doing slowly.

MAE WEST

THERE IS NO QUICK FIX

You live in a quick-fix society. Have a headache?—take an aspirin. Tired of your magazine?—turn on the television. Bored with your car?—trade it in for another.

So all in all, it's not surprising if you are looking for a quick career fix. You want to be in a better place tomorrow—no, you're prepared to be reasonable, you're willing to wait six months. But the unfortunate truth is that you won't be able to find your calling in six months. Maybe not even in six years.

Why does it take so long? Because exploration, remember, involves experiencing, reflecting, changing, experiencing, reflecting, changing, over and over again—and you can't do that in a week. Skimping on exploration guarantees a poor outcome. Only through extensive and prolonged exploring will you find your calling.

Patience, in short, is essential. By all means go for a quick fix if you wish, but please don't complain when it fails to work.

DEFERRING GRATIFICATION

Wouldn't it be great if your short-term and long-term interests coincided? Sadly, that seldom happens. All of us tend to fill much of our discretionary time with habitual activities such as blobbing out in front of television, reading magazines, or playing computer games. These are fun at a superficial level, but nobody would suggest that they are beneficial in the long term.

Your exploration will take time. That time has to come from somewhere. Almost inevitably you will need to eliminate or reduce many activities that are habitual in your life but that provide, at best, a short-term pay-off. The choice as to which activities you sacrifice is yours and yours alone, but the choice must be made.

The question is, do you have the necessary discipline? For discipline is what it takes to overcome habit.

Ready excuses for procrastination are always close at hand. Exploring, like most things that matter most in the long term, is not urgent. If it is put off until tomorrow, or next week, or next month, the world will not crash down around your ears. What's more, by its very nature it doesn't yield the quick and easy sense of progress that can come from completing short-term tasks. So the temptation always is to defer it. The danger is that you keep putting it off, not just for days and weeks, but for months and years, even decades. By then it may be too late for anything but regrets. (There is one thing that you will never regret. As Stephen Covey says, nobody was ever heard to say on their deathbed, "I wish I had spent another hour in the office.")

I have just three things to teach: simplicity, patience, compassion.
Tao Te Ching

Dost thou love life? Then do not squander time, for that is the stuff life is made of.
Benjamin Franklin

To overcome your habit of favoring short-term activities at the expense of long-term activities, you probably need to straitjacket yourself with some kind of time management system. I suggest you read a good book on the subject, like Alan Lakein's *How to Get Control of Your Time and Your Life,* or *First Things First* by Stephen Covey and Roger and Rebecca Merrill. On second thought, do more than that. Hundreds of thousands of people have read these and other time management books, enjoyed them, been persuaded by them, adopted a time management system, found that it worked—then given up on it. Habit is fearfully hard to change. Even when a new practice, such as effective time management, is manifestly good for you, it is all too easy to slip back into old, harmful habits. So simply adopting a time management system is not enough; you need to persevere with it. That is the hard part. If you are undisciplined, you will fail.

> *Bill Moyers:* But when you say you want it to be fun, you also say it requires discipline, and discipline is hard and not always fun.
>
> *Jon Kabat-Zinn:* . . . The word *discipline* has gotten a bad rap. But any athlete who wants to go to the Olympics doesn't think discipline is a bad thing.

LAZINESS

Now, let me think. What shall I do tonight? Shall I stay home, take time to reflect, confront unpleasant truths? Or shall I go to the movies?

The fact is, exploring is hard work compared with other activities that offer easy and instant gratification. So discipline is needed not just to overcome old habits but to overcome laziness, too.

As Scott Peck points out in *The Road Less Traveled,* fear is the root cause of laziness. "People find new information threatening," he writes, "because if they incorporate it they will have to do a good deal of work to revise their maps of reality, and they instinctively seek to avoid that work. . . . Their resistance is motivated by fear, yes, but the basis of their fear is laziness; it is fear of the work they would have to do. . . . They settle for the

> I've got wine, but I am too lazy to drink it; so it's just the same as if my cup were empty. I have got a lute, but am too lazy to play it; so it's just the same as if it had no strings.
>
> *Po Chui*

maintenance of a miserable status quo in preference to the tremendous amount of effort they realize will be required to work their way out of their particular traps."

DESIRE

Finding your calling, then, is a long, slow process that demands of you patience, discipline, and hard work. Now for the good news. Sustenance may be available during the years of hard slog and sacrifice.

Sorry, it's not a quick-fix potion or pill. It is desire. Mahatma Gandhi put it this way: "Only give up a thing . . . when you want some other condition so much that the thing has no longer any attraction for you, or when it seems to interfere with that which is more greatly desired."

In short, impatience, indiscipline, and indolence will be insurmountable barriers, unless ... If you want to leave your angst behind and find your bliss—*really* want it, *yearn* for it—then the hard slog and sacrifice and discipline won't seem like that at all. If you want to find your calling *that* much, then you are truly ripe for change.

"How does one become a butterfly?" she asked pensively. "You must want to fly so much that you are willing to give up being a caterpillar."

Trina Paulus

TWENTY

Money

Money does matter, more than almost anything else. Want a sound idea? Get a job now with a company with a good pension plan and a good medical plan, any company and any job, no matter how much you hate it, and stay there until you're too old to continue. That's the only way to live, by preparing to die.

JOSEPH HELLER

THE MORE ADDICTION

I know, don't tell me. You would do it if you could. You would love to explore. You would love to find your calling. But you simply can't afford to.

Neither, he tells me, can Sean. Sean is a dentist in his early forties. A good one too, as his income attests. He and his wife live in a lovely house in a classy part of town. He drives a late-model BMW. Their two children attend private schools. Their home is full of the indispensable conveniences of modern life: three televisions, two computers, two DVD players, four electric toothbrushes, a well-stocked wine cellar, a Swedish kitchen . . . they have a vacation cottage at the beach, and a boat, and membership of two golf clubs. All this and no debt.

Sean may be a rich dentist, but he's a bored one.

How many things I can do without!

Socrates
(on looking at a multitude of wares for sale)

From "The Full Alex" published by Headline. Reprinted with permission of Peattie & Taylor.

"I've had it up to here with teeth," he told me a few years ago.

"So why don't you give it up?" I asked him. "You've always talked of becoming a fishing guide one day. Why not do it now? After all, you must have built up a reasonable retirement nest egg already."

"No way," he replied. "Can't afford to stop yet. I'm not too far away, mind you. I've done my math. Just need to save a bit more. Another two or three years of hard grind, and I'll be a free man."

Well, five years have since passed and Sean is still a dentist. He's doubled his savings in the meantime, but figures that he needs "just another half million" to be on the safe side.

My prediction is that Sean will never retire from dentistry. He suffers from an addiction: Whatever he has, he will always want more. Never will he get to the point where he determines that he has enough.

> I also have in my mind that seemingly wealthy, but most terribly impoverished class of all, who have accumulated dross, but know not how to use it, or get rid of it, and thus have forged their own golden or silver fetters.
>
> *Henry David Thoreau*

THE DOCTRINE OF ENOUGH

"So what?" I hear you say sharply. "I'm nothing like Sean. His situation is quite different from mine. Even though he says otherwise, he has more than enough. But I don't."

The funny thing is, that's exactly what Sean himself said to me about his friend Arthur. Arthur wanted more, even though Sean considered that he had enough. Sean wants more, even though you consider he has enough. You want more, even though . . . well, put it this way. If you are established in a career, your income is undoubtedly above—maybe several times greater than—the national median income. At least half the population would be thrilled to earn the income that you categorize as "not enough."

"If you follow the god of More," writes Charles Handy, "you will never win. This is because there will *always* be More." Instead, you should follow the Doctrine of Enough. "The Doctrine of Enough says that if you can work out what Enough is, then and only then are you able to stop at Enough." And if you stop at Enough, you have time to pursue "the only thing that you cannot have Enough of"—personal growth.

Now, there is nothing wrong with wanting to earn a good living. Being broke is no fun. I think it was Roseanne who, paraphrasing Mae West, said, "I have been rich and miserable, and I have been poor and miserable. Believe me, rich and miserable is better." But those are not the only two choices. Look at the table below:

> Civilization, in the real sense of the term, consists not in the multiplication, but in the deliberate and voluntary reduction of wants. This alone promotes real happiness and contentment.
>
> *Mahatma Gandhi*

	Angst	Bliss
More than Enough	A1	B1
Enough	A2	B2
Less than Enough	A3	B3

Rich and miserable?—that's A1. Poor and miserable?—that's A3. Roseanne says A1 is better than A3; I guess she's right. Let's assume it's better than A2 as well. But is it better than B3? Wouldn't you rather be poor and happy than rich and miserable? And isn't B2 better still? And B1? Maybe G. K. Chesterton's Father Brown had it right

> A clear distinction must be made between our final aims—the ultimate achievements that give purpose to life—and the means through which we hope to attain them. For example, money is never a final aim; it has no value in itself. It can only act as a means, helping us to reach some ultimate goal which, to us, has inherent value.
>
> *Hans Selye*

when he said, "To be clever enough to get all that money, one must be stupid enough to want it."

For what's it's worth, my guess is that most people who are in their bliss would put themselves in the B2 zone. But their concept of Enough may be rather more modest than yours. And that's really the point. Enough is a relative value, not an absolute one. It is up to you to set it for yourself. And the lower you set it, the more scope you will have for realigning your working life in the direction of your calling.

THE JOY–MONEY TRADE-OFF

You can adopt one of two policies, each involving a trade-off. Under the first policy, you look primarily to do what will earn More; you hope to derive, as a by-product, a certain amount of joy. Under the second, you look primarily to do what will bring joy; you hope that, as a by-product, you will earn Enough.

Work as an Economic Necessity

The first policy—money before joy—sits comfortably with the prevailing notion that the purpose of working is, first and foremost, to earn a living. If you see your work primarily in economic terms, then you automatically rule out many options. No matter that these options may take you along a path rich with experience and joy—you still rule them out because they fail to meet the financial test.

In effect, you appoint a censor whose task is to apply an economic test and to expunge options that fail it. If the consequence is that you are left only with options that feed the body but starve the soul, so be it. The censor operates subtly and unconsciously. Expunged options sometimes do not even come to your awareness. By early middle age, options censored out in your teens or twenties may have been lost without a trace.

> There can be no joy of life without joy of work.
>
> *E. F. Schumacher*

To make matters worse, the less joy you glean from your work, the more insecure you become, and so the more you need money as a kind of security blanket. Hence, your need for money and the material possessions that it buys can possess you, becoming an addictive force that dictates the course of your entire career. So the More test becomes increasingly stringent. Whatever you earn, you always need More. Which is why some people who earn many times more than average still complain that they don't have Enough, yet others with a low income but an inner security consider that they do have Enough.

Work as a Biological Necessity

The second policy—joy before money—fits Hans Selye's idea that work, properly conceived, is life-giving, not life-taking, and as such a source of joy and fulfilment. If you see work as part of becoming a healthy, whole human being, you generate, through exploring, a quite different set of options that are built around all three dimensions of work: skill, enjoyment, and meaning. Financial criteria have their place, but simply to help you choose between options that meet your primary criteria.

Live to Work or Work to Live?

Said Patrick, "I don't live to work; I work to live." Asked to elaborate, he talked scornfully of some of his colleagues who worked long hours. As he saw it, they allowed their work to crowd out other activities needed to sustain family relationships and develop a balanced life. He said that, in contrast to such people, he confined work to its "proper place."

"What is the proper place?" I asked. Patrick explained that he worked simply to earn a living. His

> The question I struggled with for many years goes something like this: How can I keep my life and my work properly separated? It was the wrong question. The right question . . . is, How can I keep my life and my work properly integrated?
>
> James A. Autry

There's something inside you that knows when you're in the center, that knows when you're on the beam and off the beam. And if you get off the beam to earn money, you've lost your life. And if you stay in the center and don't get any money, you still have your bliss.

Joseph Campbell

work wasn't much fun, but at least he tried to stop it from dominating his life.

He said all this proudly, even a little piously. But his explanation betrayed the doctrine to which he subscribes: Work serves primarily an economic function. This doctrine is as life-destroying as that of the "live to work" brigade whom he decried.

Don't live to work. But don't work to live either. Work because, like breathing and eating, it is a life-nourishing activity.

When it comes to money, settle for Enough. Thereby free yourself for exploration and the chance to find your bliss. This is indeed a precious reward, one that no amount of money can buy.

TWENTY-ONE

Family

[Babbitt] stood before the covered laundry tubs, eating a chicken leg and half a saucer of raspberry jelly, and grumbling over a clammy cold boiled potato. He was thinking. It was coming to him that perhaps all life as he knew it and vigorously practiced it was futile; . . . that he hadn't much pleasure out of making money; that it was of doubtful worth to rear children merely that they might rear children who might rear children. What was it all about? What did he want?

SINCLAIR LEWIS

CLASSIC EXCUSE NUMBER TWO

"I can't afford to" is the first great excuse for failing to explore. And the second?—"Married with children." The two often go hand in hand.

James and Helen, a married couple, illustrate the point well. They are two angst-ridden people, unconsciously conspiring to perpetuate their misery. They do this because there is a reward in it for them. It suits them to have a scapegoat—in the form of each other and their children—for their continuing betrayal of their Core Selves and for the sterility of their marriage. It is always a relief to find an excuse for not confronting the ghouls.

Physically there is nothing to distinguish human society from the farm-yard except that children are more troublesome and costly than chickens and calves, and that men and women are not so completely enslaved as farm stock.

George Bernard Shaw

JAMES

> He that hath wife and children hath given hostages to fortune; for they are impediments to great enterprises, either of virtue or mischief.
>
> *Francis Bacon*

James is a successful real eatate agent. It's the old story—he has skills aplenty for this career, but derives little joy from it. He says he doesn't have Enough, which would surprise 80 percent of the population. Ask him why he needs More, and he embarks on a monologue about his wife and children. Helen, he says, is attached to a lifestyle that doesn't come cheap. She is into redecoration in a big way. She expects regular overseas vacations. She wants a new car. She wants a bigger house. Then there are the three children, aged fifteen, eleven, and eight. Their clothes cost a fortune. And they need to be educated. Pri-

© Paperlink Ltd.

Dot's spirits were lifted when, one day, her husband came home from work.

vate schools are expensive. James has to look ahead to their college years. On and on it goes. Get the picture?

Basically, James would have you believe that he nobly keeps slaving away at a career he dislikes for two reasons: to keep his wife happy, and to educate his children. Examine each reason more closely and another picture emerges.

Married . . .

Helen puts things a little differently. "James grumbles about work—always has, always will," she said to me. "But he must get something from it because why else would he work so hard? We hardly ever see him, he works most weekends, and when he *is* around, he's tired and grumpy. There has to be something to make up for all that. So yes, the money's important. It's important to James because he's into expensive things like cars and boats. And for me a decent lifestyle is the quid pro quo that makes it all bearable."

The cause-and-effect chains that the two of them describe are markedly different:

> Bigamy is having one husband too many. Monogamy is the same.
>
> *Anonymous*

JAMES'S VERSION	HELEN'S VERSION
Helen has high lifestyle expectations.	The lifestyle is compensation for his noninvolvement in family life.
▼	▲
Those are expensive.	We use the income to support our lifestyle.
▼	▲
I have to come up with the money.	He earns a good income.
▼	▲
I have to work hard.	He chooses to work hard.
▼	▲
I have to stick with a career I dislike.	He puts work before family.
▼	▲
I have little time left over for family matters.	James isn't interested in family matters.

What it comes down to is this. James claims that he wouldn't work so hard if Helen would settle for a less expensive lifestyle. And Helen claims that she would settle for a less expensive lifestyle if James wouldn't work so hard. It would be comic if it weren't tragic.

. . . with Children

James has worked too hard throughout the years of his marriage to have had much to do with the children. When they were young, they were usually asleep by the time he arrived home. Now that they are older, he is a little more involved in their lives, but his relationship with them remains proper rather than warm. Sometimes he feels that the core of the family consists of Helen and the children—that he is simply on the fringe. That is not to say that his children don't matter to him. They do. He wishes he were closer to them.

Once I asked him what hopes he held for Allan, the oldest child, about whom he often talks proudly. "Well," he replied, "I don't really care. That's up to him. I just want him to be his own man." He seemed quite oblivious to the irony that he role-models precisely the opposite behavior.

As to the children's education, James makes two glib assumptions: that private school education is in their best interests, and that he needs to sustain his present income to pay for it. Some would question the first assumption, but let's give James the benefit of the doubt. The second assumption simply does not stand up to scrutiny. Clearly there is a point at which, if the household income fell, private school fees could no longer be afforded. But where is that point? Is it an income cut of five thousand dollars? Ten thousand? Twenty? More than that? The simple fact is, James doesn't know. He has never done the math. He has never sat down with Helen to consider what lifestyle sacrifices they would be willing to make to sustain private schooling. And he won't.

Sometimes careers resemble long-standing marriages in which passion is exchanged for comfort, security, and predictability in an uncertain world. . . . For every day we don't strive to live authentically we do pay a price, with compounded interest.

Sarah Ban Breathnach

He has let himself be persuaded that if he leaves for work earlier in the morning and comes home more tired at night, he is proving how devoted he is to his family by expending himself to provide them with all the things they have seen advertised.

Harold Kushner

Because it suits him just fine to have another scapegoat to justify his failure to explore.

For the same reason, James won't ever challenge a third glib assumption he makes. Private school education may be of great benefit to his children. But something else would benefit them even more: having a father who saw plenty of them, knew them well, and was deeply involved in their upbringing. If a choice needed to be made—if the kids could have either private schooling or an involved dad, but not both—every child development expert would opt for the latter. But James prefers to assume that the former matters more.

HELEN

Helen, a marketing graduate, worked for a manufacturer until her late twenties as a member of the sales team. She didn't enjoy it much, but who said work was meant to be fun? Six months into her first pregnancy, she quit with a sigh of relief. She hasn't had a paid job in the sixteen years since.

She used to say she would resume work once she no longer had preschoolers at home. Now she says she would resume work if she could find a suitable job. The problem, she says, is the children: She would need a job with flexible work hours so that she could be at home after school and during the school vacations, but "clearly" any job that met her needs in terms of hours would be menial and low paid. So she has not attempted to find work.

It is not that Helen is idle. Besides being heavily involved with the children's school activities, she is a champion shopper, plays tennis and golf, and mixes with a circle of close friends. Then of course there is the house and garden to maintain. This lifestyle would be fine, if she enjoyed it. Unfortunately she doesn't. She is bored, and it shows. She wishes she could reestablish a

These poor people live an uninteresting life together—they sacrifice their joy and adventures to money—and the money merely enables them to live for more dull plodding—to bring more people into the world so that the same old futile work and sorrow may be carried on for another span of years.

Joseph Campbell

career of some sort. But when any options within her fields of interest are discussed with her, she dismisses them as either beyond or beneath her capabilities.

Helen sometimes thinks that her bliss may be something to do with art or design. But she won't explore within that domain. She could have made a start a few months ago when, through a friend, she had the chance to take up a part-time job in the art gallery's bookshop. This would have been a superb point of entry into the domain. Initially the prospect excited her, but then she came up with excuses not to accept. The family would suffer. The work would be "menial." And the pay on offer was "lousy."

BACK TO BASICS

James and Helen blame each other and the children for their inertia, but clearly they could explore if so minded. What would exploring mean? A gradual realignment accomplished over many years—not, as James chooses to assume, immediate, dramatic change and a plummeting income.

The starting point would be to ask, singly and jointly (and perhaps helped by a counselor), basic questions that they are currently ignoring. Not just questions relating specifically to work (including skill-enjoyment-meaning questions), but questions about their whole life. *What really matters to us? What are our values? What are our priorities? Do we want to keep growing? Is it important to us to breathe new life into our stale marriage? How important? What are we willing to do to bring this about? How much do we want to find fulfilling work? What is most important in terms of the children's development? What material sacrifices are we prepared to make? What is Enough?*

Most important, though, is to keep working; I knew that I essentially never wanted *not* to work. To me, working is a form of sustenance, like food or water, and nearly as essential.

Katharine Graham

They had just about everything they wanted in terms of material goods, but were not really living. They were not truly free. They wanted to step out and make a difference, they wanted to contribute, but they were immobilized by fear and by the need to have more and more material goods. It was the need to "have" instead of to "be."

Joseph Jaworski

CONSTRAINTS, NOT BARRIERS

Your goal is to fashion a working life that fits the person you really are; and that person has, and cherishes, a family. In developing your working life, you can no more disregard that fact than you could, say, your skill base. It is real; it is a part of the totality that is you.

Shucking off your family to seek your calling is the last thing you want to do. But it is equally absurd to act as if you are a prisoner to your family.

Family circumstances give rise to constraints; there's no denying that. And yes, they are often substantial constraints. (James and Helen share their reluctance to explore. A situation even more deserving of compassion is where one partner wants to explore, but the other is uninterested.) In the final analysis, however, they are just constraints; they are not insurmountable barriers.

All of life has to be conducted within constraints. Exploration is not exempt from that. Indeed, it is one of the reasons why your exploring is likely to take many years. The need to learn more about yourself, the need for security, the need for income—all of these are constraints. Grappling with such constraints is at the heart of exploration.

Family commitments are simply another constraint. The ghouls want you to believe otherwise. They will seek to persuade you that a snare of family obligations entraps you and leaves you no choice but to stick with the career that is giving you so much angst. Don't let them succeed. Only you can imprison yourself.

Whatever your family circumstances, adopt the explorer's mind-set. If you do, you will discover that by a succession of small steps undertaken over a decade, you can indeed transform your working life.

> For a long time it had seemed to me that life was about to begin—real life. But there was always some obstacle in the way, something to be got through first, some unfinished business, time still to be served, a debt to be paid. Then life would begin. At last it dawned on me that these obstacles were my life.
>
> *Alfred D'Souza*

The Opportunities

Stanley was deeply disappointed when, high in the Tibetan mountains, he finally found his true self.

TWENTY-TWO

Talent

One day, a long, long time ago at a retail music store where I had been working for almost a year, I had an unexpected revelation. As I stood next to the cash register, the sky seemed to suddenly open up over my head and a throng of beautiful angels came flying down and swirled around me. In glorious, lilting tones, their voices rang out, "You haaaaate your job, you haaaaate your job . . ." And then they left. But I knew it was true—angels don't lie. I hated my job.

GARY LARSON (*FAR SIDE* CARTOONIST)

THE HEAVENLY AD AGENCY

Imagine the creative team of the celestial ad agency, working on the campaign to promote the amazing new laundry powder Snibbo. Over there, working on the finished art, is Matisse. T. S. Eliot is the copywriter. Stravinsky is putting the finishing touches on the musical ditties. With talents like those on the job, it will surely be an ad campaign made in heaven.

But there's a problem. Matisse, Eliot, and Stravinsky seem, well, a bit off form. Their work is good, but not up to the caliber of which we know they are capable. If only we could find a way to unleash their true talents . . .

He is not only idle who does nothing, but he is idle who might be better employed.

Socrates

TALENT BLINDNESS

You may not know it, but you are talented. Why do I assert that with such absolute conviction? We'll come to that soon. But first, let's consider why it is that you may be blind to your own talents.

For a start, you may make the common mistake of confusing "talent" with "genius." Genius is talent with a capital T. It is solid-gold, diamond-studded talent. Okay, so you may not have genius—but you still have talent.

Or you may reserve the word *talent* for the fields of culture or sports. You may talk readily of talented artists, writers, and football players, but never of talented auditors, plumbers, or typists. You may indeed see celebrity status as a touchstone of talent. It is not.

Perhaps you're a victim of the natural human tendency to take for granted what you have. If you have the ability to do something easily, you may assume that everyone else can do it easily, too, and hence fail to recognize it as a special ability.

But usually the chief cause of talent blindness is a lack of self-knowledge. If you don't know yourself well, you probably lack self-esteem. You may be excellent at acknowledging your own weaknesses, but oblivious to your own innate strengths. And so you move through life tragically unaware of your own talents.

> I was the prototype of the "successful" individual who had worked for years and years . . . only to look up after twenty years and realize that he never had understood his true purpose for being here, and was not truly stepping into his own life. There was so much wasted talent around, so much hidden talent, and what I wanted to do was help discover and develop that talent.
>
> Joseph Jaworski

WHAT TALENTS ARE

What exactly are these things called "talents"? According to the *Oxford English Dictionary*, a talent is simply "a special natural ability or aptitude." *Webster's Dictionary* says something similar: Talent consists of "the natural endowments of a person" or "a special often creative or artistic aptitude."

Focus now on two words in these definitions: *special* and *natural*. Together they capture the essence.

Special means "out of the ordinary." Your talents are abilities or aptitudes that most other people don't have to the same extent. More about this shortly.

Natural means "innate," as opposed to "acquired." Your talents derive from your Core Self. They existed from the moment of conception. They may have been developed since birth, but they have not been acquired since birth.

It is because talents are sourced in the Core Self that their exercise is fundamentally an intuitive process. Woody Allen, for example, said in a television interview that jokes bubble out of him spontaneously. When he says something funny, he himself laughs because, just like the audience, he is hearing it for the first time.

In similar vein, Timothy Gallwey observes in *The Inner Game of Tennis* that someone who is playing tennis well invariably has a sort of "mindlessness," in the sense that he or she is not thinking about each movement but, rather, moving on automatic pilot. Gallwey suggests some gamesmanship to test this theory: "The next time your opponent is having a hot streak, simply ask him as you switch courts, 'Say, George, what are you doing so differently that's making your forehand so good today?' If he takes the bait—and 95 percent will—and begins to think about how he is swinging, telling you how he's really meeting the ball out in front, keeping his wrist firm and following through better, his streak will invariably end. He will lose his timing and fluidity as he tries to repeat what he has just told you he was doing so well."

The enemy, in Gallwey's thesis, is what he calls Self 1: the conscious, thinking, analyzing, critical part of the mind. Somehow Self 1 has to be distracted so that Self 2— the unconscious, doing, intuitive, natural self, the place where your talents reside—is free to perform without interference.

> You will ask me whence I take my ideas? That I cannot say with any degree of certainty; they come to me uninvited, directly or indirectly. I could almost grasp them in my hands, out in Nature's open, in the woods, during my promenades, in the silence of the night, at the earliest dawn. They are roused by moods which in the poet's case are transmitted into words, and in mine into tones; that sound, roar and storm until at last they take shape for me as notes.
>
> *Beethoven*

DO *YOU* HAVE TALENTS?

> Nature never repeats her-
> self and the possibilities of
> one human soul will never
> be found in another.
>
> *Elizabeth Cady Stanton*

Probably you're prepared to accept that every human being, yourself included, has innate abilities or aptitudes. But are any of yours special? This is where, through lack of self-knowledge, you may answer no, and thus justify the conclusion that you have no talents. If so, you're dead wrong.

As we have seen in chapter 4, your Core Self consists of a bundle of potentialities waiting to be realized. They include a diverse range of abilities and aptitudes.

How diverse? Well, think about your face alone. It is a unique synthesis of countless variables. Indeed, each individual feature of your face is itself such a synthesis. Your eyes, to take just one simple example, are a synthesis of limitless variables relating to shape, color, and placement—and that's before we even get to the variables relating to the eye's functionality. In effect, your face is a unique synthesis of unique syntheses.

That's just the face. Now think of the variables relating to other far more complex parts of your being—abstract thinking, analytical thinking, language, spatial reasoning, empathy, numerical calculation, emotions, sexuality, tonal sensitivity . . . the list goes on and on.

> Each of us comes equipped
> with enough raw ability
> across the board to achieve
> that seemingly rare and
> mysterious state we call
> mastery in some mode of
> thought and expression,
> some interpersonal and
> entrepreneurial enterprise,
> some art or craft.
>
> *George Leonard*

The scope for diversity and variability is underlined by the work done by Howard Gardner. We are accustomed to thinking of intelligence as a single, monolithic commodity, one whose ration within a given individual is revealed by his or her ability with words or numbers. Nature has, we think, dished out this commodity lavishly to some people; they have a "high IQ" and are therefore "intelligent." Others who have received a meager helping have a "low IQ"; they are unintelligent. Everyone sits somewhere along this continuum.

A nice theory, but wrong, as Gardner demonstrates

in *Frames of Mind* and *Creating Minds.* Having studied people with severe brain damage, he contends persuasively that there are at least seven different intelligences: linguistic, logical-mathematical, artistic, musical, kinesthetic (that is, physical), intrapersonal, and interpersonal. Note that only the first two of these directly involve the ability to manipulate words or numbers.

Gardner's studies show that the multiple intelligences are not necessarily linked: You might be a genius at one and lousy at all the rest. The philosophy professor who constantly trips over her own feet is no more entitled to be called intelligent than the inarticulate but skillful football player. The physicist who can't hold a tune is no more entitled to be called intelligent than the bass guitarist who can't remember his seven times table.

All this serves to underline the point: The particular set of potentialities making up your Core Self is a unique permutation. The synthesis of syntheses that is found in you is found in nobody else. That is why it is certain that you have innate abilities that are special. That is why it is certain that you have talents.

TALENT AS SYNTHESIS

Just as, on analysis, the apparent unity of the generic quality called "intelligence" dissolves into many parts, so does that of any talent you care to name. A talent is a point of intersection. It is a coming together of many different attributes. It is an integration of disparate elements.

Let's take a relatively straightforward sporting talent as an example: playing golf. You might think it safe to assume that golf's all-time legends—Bobby Jones, Jack Nicklaus, Tiger Woods, and the like—shared a talent for hitting a golf ball. But it's not that simple. Expert observers seeking to explain the greatness of each of

> My business is not to remake myself,
> But make the absolute best of what God made.
> *Robert Browning*

> There is no substitute for talent. Industry and all the virtues are of no avail.
> *Aldous Huxley*

From "The Full Alex" published by Headline. Reprinted with permission of Peattie & Taylor.

them cite an extraordinary range of different factors. Chin position. Feet placement. Grip. Hip turn. Weight transfer. Elbow straightness. Wrist cock. Takeaway. Backswing. Follow-through. Fortitude. Analytical ability. Competitiveness. Patience. Emotional control. Aspects of all these factors and a hundred others are variously described as crucial to the success of one great golfer or another. Suddenly that generic description of a talent—"hitting a golf ball"—seems utterly simplistic.

What are we to conclude? First, being able to hit a golf ball well is a synthesis of numerous elements. Second, the mix of those elements differs from golfer to golfer. Third, being a great golfer is a synthesis of many elements over and above those needed to hit a golf ball well. And fourth, again the mix of those elements differs from golfer to golfer.

What is true of hitting a golf ball is true of any talent. When scrutinized, it reveals itself to be a potpourri of diverse elements. In no two people is the mixture the same. In that very real sense, no two people have the same talent. The talents that reside in you are truly unique to you.

It is because every talent is a synthesis that its exercise is inherently a creative process. The link between creativity and synthesis was captured by Ayn Rand in these words: "All work is an act of creating and comes from the same source: from an inviolate capacity to see through one's own eyes . . . which means: the capacity to see, to connect

The voyage of discovery lies not in seeking new vistas but in having new eyes.

Marcel Proust

and to make what had not been seen, connected and made before." Are you one of those people who say that they are not creative? If so, you are mistaken. Every time you use your talents, you are performing an act of creativity.

FINDING THE INTERSECTION

So yes, you undoubtedly have talents. But do you know what they are? If not, you know what you have to do. Yes—explore!

The key to the search lies in a word used often in this chapter: *synthesis*. Look for the points of intersection. I know of a child who loved to draw. But he didn't become an artist. He had another love. It was, in his own words, "biology and, more specifically, when placed in a common jar, which of two organisms would devour the other." But he didn't become a biologist either. He was a funny boy who could make other children laugh. But no, he didn't become a comedian. What did he become? No prizes if you have guessed already. I'm talking about *Far Side* cartoonist Gary Larson. The talent? It was not drawing by itself or biology by itself or comedy by itself. It was drawing funny pictures about animals.

> I don't think for a moment that a child is a *tabula rasa*, an empty page that life experiences and culture make into a person. Clearly, a child is fully present in that moment of birth, and what happens later is simply an unfolding and unwrapping of a complicated and rich destiny and potentiality.
>
> *Thomas Moore*

TALENT AND CHARACTER

Your talents come from your Core Self. To be unleashed, therefore, they must be aligned with other aspects of your Core Self. Despite all the training and development in the world, they will still be shackled unless deployed in the service of what is your bliss.

This nexus between unleashing your talents and expressing your essential character is fundamental. You simply can't develop your talents to their potential without developing your whole person. Gary Player, one of the greatest of all golfers, was so conscious of this that he sought deliberately to improve himself as a golfer by improving himself as a person. It is for this reason that he attributed much of his golfing success to four books: the Bible, *The Power of Positive Thinking, Imitations of Christ,* and *Yoga and Health.*

Tragically, technical training often ignores this critical feature of talent. A talented student may be taught to mimic the technical skills of teachers or past masters. Inevitably, the antiseptic focus on technique at the expense of character stunts development of the talent.

Now you will understand why Matisse, Eliot, and Stravinsky are doomed to perform below potential in the celestial ad agency. Snibbo may indeed be a superb new soap powder, but writing ads for it has no meaning for them, and brings them little enjoyment. They are in what we have called a Wallenda career (see pages 66–67). If they want to unleash their talents, there is only one way: They will need to deploy them in their calling.

THE MERIT SYNDROME

Your talents were born, not made. They were given to you by nature or by God (which explains why they are sometimes called gifts). They represent the purest, highest form of your humanness. If you deploy them in the domain of your bliss, they will bring you vitality, joy, and fulfillment.

Yet how many people do deploy them in this way, or even recognize them? A disease—merit syndrome—plagues the developed world. It causes a focus not on talents but on certain skills—those related to verbal and numerical reasoning. It is little wonder if children come to see having a logical mind as a higher virtue than having a creative mind. And so they are set on a path that leads inexorably to careers that are practical and finan-

What drives me on is the excitement that music can breed; it's the prospect of getting more and more people interested in what I love. Playing safe and hiding within the classical traditions is a much bigger gamble for me because within that route is almost certain death to the spirit.

Nigel Kennedy

cially sound and for which they are equipped with the necessary intellectual skills. One dimension gets overlooked: What really makes this unique individual tick? What truly stirs him? What are her passions?

This celebration of skills instead of talents is a tragedy. Most of us go through life blind to our talents, or with at best a dim awareness. Even if we do recognize a talent, we usually give it little space in our lives. We might indulge it occasionally through a hobby. But all too often we fail even to do that.

What a waste! As individuals, we waste the opportunity to lead fulfilling lives in place of the gray, anonymous lives that so many of us endure. As a society, we waste the opportunity to derive the fruits that the exercise of talent creates.

> If he has a talent and learns somehow to use the whole of it, he has gloriously succeeded, and won a satisfaction and a triumph few men know.
>
> *Thomas Wolfe*

UNLEASHING *YOUR* TALENTS

And you? If you are highly skilled at what you do, so-called success may come your way. But unless you unleash your talents, security and happiness will continue to elude you. On the other hand, express your talents in your calling and you will derive far more fulfillment than any career "success" can bring.

As we have already seen, "follow your bliss" and "pursue your calling" are synonymous. Now we have discovered a third way of saying the same thing: "Unleash your talents." The three can be put together—indeed, synthesized—in nine short words:

DISCOVER BLISS BY UNLEASHING YOUR TALENTS IN YOUR CALLING.

> This . . . is the only real problem of life, the only worthwhile preoccupation of man: What is one's true talent, his secret gift, his authentic vocation? In what way is one truly unique, and how can he express this uniqueness, give it form, dedicate it to something beyond himself?
>
> *Ernest Becker*

TWENTY-THREE

Contribution

Bill Moyers: *In this sense, unlike heroes like Prometheus or Jesus, we're not going on our journey to save the world but to save ourselves.*

Joseph Campbell: *But in doing that, you save the world! The influence of a vital person vitalizes, there's no doubt about it. The world without spirit is a wasteland. . . . Any world is a valid world if it's alive. The thing to do is to bring life to it, and the only way to do that is to find in your own case where the life is and become alive yourself.*

UNIQUE AND UNIVERSAL

I've said it before and I'll say it again: You're one of a kind. As I put it in the last chapter, you're a unique synthesis of unique syntheses. No other person who has ever walked this planet is the same as you.

The differences aren't just skin deep. At your very core you see, feel, experience life, differently from everybody else.

And yet . . . are you and I *that* different?

What we have in common far exceeds our differences. We both have eyes, a nose, a mouth, we both have a liver and kidneys, we both have a mind and a heart. We are both humans.

No man is an island,
  entire of itself;
Every man is a piece of
  the continent, a part of
  the main . . .
Any man's death
  diminishes me, because
  I am involved in
  Mankind;
And therefore, never send
  to know for whom the
  bell tolls;
It tolls for thee.

John Donne

197

Biologists tell us that you are, in fact, my cousin. You and I share ancestors. There's a fair chance that the most recent of them lived just a few hundred years ago.

Sages of all faiths down the ages go farther. They say that if you and I were to expand our consciousness through meditation and prayer, all the apparent differences between us would dissolve. They say we would then perceive a new reality: that instead of being separate individuals, we are one, that you are I and I am you.

Sky Water

> The paradoxical fact is that the deeper I experience my own or another's unique individuality, the clearer I see through myself and him the reality of universal man.
>
> *Erich Fromm*

Here then is the paradox. You are a distinct individual, unique and encouraged in this book to assert that uniqueness by following your calling. And yet at the same time you are not distinct but part of a universal oneness that embraces all humankind.

As I write these words, I am sitting alone on a deserted beach, pad on my knee. It is a perfectly still midsummer evening. Before me stretches out a vast mirror—the calm surface of a lake, its unruffled tranquillity disturbed only by feeding cormorants.

The sky is a quilt. Clouds—purple, gray, and white, some towering upward, dense and thick, others floating like a filmy veil—break up the azure. All this is reflected in the mirror before me. I look across the water to my left and am hypnotized by a play of color and pattern. I look to my right and a new play, quite different but no less mesmerizing, greets me. If I then look back to the left, my eyes feast on a different show yet. A thousand images, each unique, dance before me as I slowly turn my head.

Each image unique. Yet each image a reflection of the one sky.

> I am large; I contain multitudes.
>
> *Walt Whitman*

Just as the lake before me reflects the same heavens in a thousand different ways, so you and I, in our own unique ways, reflect our common humanity.

HELPING ME BY HELPING YOURSELF

I have urged you in this book to follow your bliss into your calling. But you may think that to do so would be selfish. If so, then don't do it for yourself. Do it for me. Do it for humanity.

How am *I* helped by *your* being true to your Core Self and following your calling?

You Breathe Life into Me

The world is crowded with people who are alienated from their Core Selves and blind to their talents; people who needlessly endure drab, sterile, conventional half-lives.

By eschewing falseness and being true to yourself, you vitalize yourself. In so doing, you radiate an energy that helps to vitalize me and the world we share.

You Create for Me

You are different from me. When you assert the uniqueness of your Core Self, you see things that I cannot see, connect things that I cannot connect. And in so doing, you create new awareness, new knowledge, new ideas, new expressions, new objects.

What you create benefits the world. And it benefits me.

You Teach Me

I need contrast to make me aware. Without night, I would not know what day is. Without wet, I would not know what dry is. Without pain, I would not know what joy is.

In the same way, I need the contrast between you and me so that I may know who I am. By being not a drab clone but truly your unique self, you impart learning in me about myself that I could get from nobody else.

Claude Monet lived in Giverny for thirty-five years, painting the same water lilies year after year in each new day's light. To look with the freshness of eyes that see today's light anew—this is the beginner's mind.

Jack Kornfield

You Inspire Me

I often settle for mediocrity. I lower my sights. I fumble around in the dark. By deploying your talents, you turn on the light and remind me how awe-inspiring is the humanity we share.

In 1976 I sat transfixed in front of the television, bewitched by the balance and grace of a twelve-year-old Romanian gymnast, Nadia Comaneci. The world watched with me. In 2000 the same thing happened again, only this time it was the power and poise of Marion Jones on the sprint track that captivated.

Nadia Comaneci and Marion Jones unleashed talents that had a primal source at the very core of their being. By pushing their talents to the limits, they gave expression to the purest, highest form of their humanness. I was able to exalt with them because their deeds spoke about what it is to be human.

You Connect with Me

The experience of being alive is often a lonely struggle. I erect facades and don't know how to pull them down. But you, by being true and honest, burst through the facades and make me feel once again real and connected.

Nigel Kennedy was once playing Brahms's Violin Concerto as part of a television documentary. There had been, inevitably, takes and retakes, which meant that for the whole day he had been immersed in the composition. His manager watched as "Nigel ventured off again into this section of the concerto. That astonishing, faraway look returned to his face immediately. . . . After a while we realized the situation was changing and Nigel's face was registering more and more emotion. As the music finished the room went silent. . . . He was so moved by the music he'd been playing for the last ten hours that tears had welled up in his eyes. . . . He made an awkward remark to me, almost apologetically, to the effect that he

> The Beatles tapped into the deepest, truest aspects of being human. And in so doing, they, like all great artists, put the rest of us in touch with the divine.
>
> *Mark Hertsgaard*

> Close! Stand close to me, Starbuck; let me look into a human eye; it is better than to gaze into sea or sky; better than to gaze upon God. By the green land; by the bright hearthstone! this is the magic glass, man; I see my wife and my child in thine eye.
>
> *Herman Melville*

couldn't help it, for without an orchestra over his shoulder to worry about, he had got lost in the music."

What was happening here? Brahms and Kennedy were connecting. When Brahms had composed his concerto, he had sought simply to express, as truthfully and intimately as he could, his own feelings. But by doing so he entered into communion with another who lived in a different country more than a century later.

IN PRAISE OF SELF-CENTEREDNESS

I recall reading somewhere a lovely story of Mother Teresa of Calcutta. We think of her as the personification of selflessness. But no, she served others so magnificently because her Core Self found its bliss in the service of God. Anyway, when she was setting up a hospice in New York, a well-meaning group of matrons donated brand-new carpets. She didn't want the carpets; they simply weren't part of her vision for the hospice. On the other hand, if she didn't accept them, feelings would be hurt. So what did she do? You and I might have agonized—not Mother Teresa. She point-blank refused to accept the carpets. No way was she going to betray her truths to spare the feelings of the benefactors.

> When someone asked Gandhi how he could so continually sacrifice himself for India, he replied, "I do this for myself alone."
>
> *Jack Kornfield*

[She was] self-centered in the best possible way: *being centered in the truth of who she was.* Her Authentic Self.

Sarah Ban Breathnach

The accusation "selfish" is often thrown at people who seek to be true to themselves. But which, I ask you, is the conduct that is deserving of this tag? Is it to use your talents to bring yourself fully alive, knowing that by so doing you will be bringing vitality, creativity, learning, and connection to sterile, empty, and isolated lives? Or is it to lock those talents away and become a slave to convention, thereby denying both yourself and others of their life-giving properties?

Sitting beside Walden Pond, Henry David Thoreau came to understand this idea that it is by being who you truly are, and being so *for yourself,* that you can best do good for others. The usual worthy advice, he observed, is that you should "with kindness aforethought go about doing good." This is wrong: Instead of going about *doing* good, you should set about *being* good by following the particular path that is right for you. The sun, he pointed out, does not try to do good, going about "like Robin Goodfellow, peeping in at every cottage window, inspiring lunatics, and tainting meats, and making darkness visible"; instead it goes about "the world in his own orbit, doing it good, or rather, as a truer philosophy has discovered, the world going about him getting good." (In a similar vein, Buckminster Fuller noted that the bee doesn't pollinate flowers; it just gets honey.)

Mahatma Gandhi. Joan of Arc. Thomas Edison. Emily Pankhurst. St. Thomas Aquinas. Marie Curie. Copernicus. Boadicea. Socrates. Jane Austen. Alexander the Great. Florence Nightingale. Leonardo da Vinci. Eleanor Roosevelt. Who among them devoted their lives to obediently fitting in, doing what was expected of them, subjugating their own preferences, serving the will of others, meekly following the conventions of the day?

The fact is that all of them founded their lives on the dictates of their inner selves. They were, in the best sense of the term, self-centered. And thank God they

Those who achieve growth not only enjoy the fruits of growth but give the same fruits to the world. Evolving as individuals, we carry humanity on our backs. And so humanity evolves.

M. Scott Peck

were. Because the progress and renewal of humankind depends on such individuals who, in honoring their Core Selves, buck the system, cut their own path, make new rules, and create new values.

That is why I implore *you* to be self-centered, too. Honor your Core Self. Follow your bliss. Unleash your talents.

Pursue your calling. And by so doing enrich humanity.

Life is no brief candle for me. It's a sort of splendid torch which I've got to hold up for the moment and I want to make it burn as brightly as possible before handing it on to future generations.

George Bernard Shaw

The following organizations and individuals were kind enough to give permission for
the reproduction of cartoons:
Andrew Mann Limited, London, United Kingdom: cartoons from *Alex* (pages 25, 58,
123, 157, 172, and 192).
The Bulletin with Newsweek, Sydney, Australia: the cartoon by Flak on page 75.
David Fletcher, Auckland, New Zealand: the cartoons by him on pages 15, 103,
and 151.
John Guaspari, Massachusetts, USA: the cartoon by Dick Vieira and John Guaspari on
page 113.
Paperlink Limited, London, United Kingdom: the cartoons on page 178 and 185.
Punch, London, United Kingdom: the cartoon on page 168.
Harley Schwadron, Michigan, USA: the cartoon by him on page 1.
United Media, USA: cartoons from *Dilbert* (pages 7, 45, 92, 107, 116, and 142).
Universal Press Syndicate: cartoons from *Calvin and Hobbes,* pages 31, 71, 131, 138,
161, and 201, and *Doonesbury* (pages 50 and 81).

I would like to acknowledge with gratitude all of the writers I have quoted from. An
exhaustive search was done to determine whether previously published material
included in this book required permission to reprint. If there has been an error, I
apologize; a correction will be published in subsequent editions.
The following authors and publishers were kind enough to grant permission to
include excerpts from:
The Power of Myth by Joseph Campbell and Bill Moyers, copyright © 1988 by Apos-
trophe S Productions, Inc. and Bill Moyers and Alfred Van der Marck Editions,
Inc. for itself and the estate of Joseph Campbell. Used by permission of Doubleday,
a division of Random House, Inc.
The Hungry Spirit by Charles Handy, copyright © 1998 by Charles Handy. Used by
permission of The Random House Group Ltd.
The Age of Unreason by Charles Handy, copyright © 1989 by Charles Handy. Used by
permission of The Random House Group Ltd.
Waiting for the Mountain to Move by Charles Handy, copyright © 1991 by Charles
Handy. Used by permission of The Random House Group Ltd.
The Empty Raincoat by Charles Handy, copyright © 1994 by Charles Handy. Used by
permission of The Random House Group Ltd.
Beyond Uncertainty by Charles Handy, copyright © 1995 by Charles Handy. Used by
permission of The Random House Group Ltd.

Bibliography

Alighieri, Dante. *The Divine Comedy.* Trans. Lawrence Grant White. New York: Pantheon, 1948.

Allen, Woody. *Death.* New York: S. French, 1975.

Alvarez, A. *Feeding the Rat.* New York: Atlanta Monthly Press, 1989.

Arron, Deborah L. *Running from the Law.* Berkeley: Ten Speed Press, 1991.

Augustine, Dennis. *Invisible Means of Support.* San Francisco: Golden Gate Publications, 1994.

Autry, James A. *Love and Work.* New York: William Morrow, 1994.

Becker, Ernest. *The Denial of Death.* New York: Free Press, 1973.

Beckett, Samuel. *Waiting for Godot.* New York: Chelsea House, 1987.

Bennis, Warren, and Burt Nanus. *Leaders.* New York: Harper & Row, 1985.

Bland, Alexander. *The Nureyev Image.* New York: Galahad Books, 1981.

Blofeld, John. *The Wheel of Life.* London: Rider, 1972.

Bohm, David. *Wholeness and the Implicate Order.* London: Routledge Paul, 1980.

Branden, Nathaniel. "Passion and Soulfulness." In *Handbook for the Soul* edited by Richard Carlson and Benjamin Shield. New York: Doubleday, 1996.

Breathnach, Sarah Ban. *Simple Abundance: A Daybook of Comfort and Joy.* New York: Warner Books, 1995.

———. *Something More: Excavating Your Authentic Self.* New York: Warner Books, 1998.

Bridges, William. *Creating You & Co.* Reading: Addison-Wesley, 1997.

Brion, Marcel. *Cézanne.* New York: Simon & Schuster, 1988.

Butler, Samuel. *The Way of All Flesh.* New York: Alfred A. Knopf, 1993.

Campbell, Joseph. *The Hero with a Thousand Faces.* Princeton: Princeton University Press, 1972.

———. *Myths to Live By.* New York: Penguin Arkana, 1993.

Campbell, Joseph, with Bill Moyers. *The Power of Myth.* New York: Main Street Books, 1988.

Canfield, Jack, and Jacqueline Miller, eds. *Heart at Work.* New York: McGraw-Hill, 1998.

Capra, Fritjof. *The Tao of Physics.* New York: Bantam, 1977.

———. *The Turning Point.* New York: Bantam Doubleday Dell, 1988.

Castanada, Carlos. *The Teachings of Don Juan.* Berkeley: University of California Press, 1972.

Chesterton, G. K. "Paradise of Thieves." In *The Father Brown Omnibus.* New York: Dodd, Mead, 1983.

Clark, Kenneth. *Another Part of the Wood.* London: J. Murray, 1974.

Cook, Peter, and Dudley Moore. *Dud & Pete—The Dagenham Dialogues.* London: Methuen, 1971.

Copeland, Aaron. *Music and Imagination.* Charles Eliot Norton Lectures, 1951–52. Cambridge: Harvard University Press, 1952.

Covey, Stephen R., and Roger and Rebecca Merrill. *First Things First.* New York: Simon & Schuster, 1994.

Dalai Lama, the, and Howard Cutler. *The Art of Happiness.* New York: Riverhead Books, 1998.

Dass, Ram. *Be Here Now.* New York: Crown Publishing, 1971.

Davies, Paul. *God and the New Physics.* New York: Touchstone Books, 1984.

Davies, Paul, and John Gribbin. *The Matter Myth.* New York: Touchstone Books, 1992.

Davies, Paul. *The Mind of God.* New York: Touchstone Books, 1993.

Dawkins, Richard. *The Blind Watchmaker.* New York: W. W. Norton, 1996.

———. *River Out of Eden.* New York: Basic Books, 1996.

Dennett, Daniel C. *Darwin's Dangerous Idea.* New York: Simon & Schuster, 1994.

Drucker, Peter. *Managing for the Future.* New York: Dutton, 1992.

———. *Post-Capitalist Society.* New York: HarperCollins, 1993.

———. *Managing in a Time of Great Change.* New York: Plume, 1998.

Emerson, Ralph Waldo. *Self-Reliance.* New York: Dover Publications, 1993.

Erikson, Erik. *Childhood and Society.* New York: W. W. Norton, 1993.

Evans, Paul, and Fernando Bartolomé. *Must Success Cost So Much?* London: Grant McIntyre, 1980.

Feynman, Richard. *The Pleasure of Finding Things Out.* Cambridge: Perseus Publishing, 2000.

Fischer, Louis. *Gandhi: His Life and Message for the World.* New York: Mentor, 1954.

Fonteyn, Margot. *Autobiography.* New York: Warner Books, 1977.

Fox, Matthew. *The Reinvention of Work.* San Francisco: Harper San Francisco, 1994.

Frankl, Viktor E. *Man's Search for Meaning.* New York: Washington Square Press, 1985.

Fromm, Erich. *The Art of Being.* New York: Continuum, 1992.

Frost, Nina. *Soul Mapping.* New York: Marlowe & Co., 2000.

Frost, Robert. *The Complete Poems of Robert Frost.* New York: Henry Holt, 1949.

Gallwey, W. Timothy. *The Inner Game of Tennis.* New York: Random House, 1997.

Gardner, Howard. *Frames of Mind.* New York: Basic Books, 1983.

———. *Creating Minds.* New York: Basic Books, 1993.

———. *Leading Minds.* New York: Basic Books, 1995.

Gibran, Kahlil. "On Work." In *The Prophet.* New York: Random House, 1976.

Gilder, George. *Microcosm: The Quantum Revolution in Economics and Technology.* New York: Simon & Schuster, 1989.

Godden, Rumer. *A House with Four Rooms.* New York: William Morrow, 1989.

Goodall, Jane. *Reason for Hope.* New York: Warner Books, 2000.

Gould, Stephen Jay. *Dinosaur in a Haystack.* New York: Harmony Books, 1995.

Graham, Katharine. *Personal History.* New York: Vintage Books, 1998.

Halberstam, David. *Playing for Keeps: Michael Jordan and the World He Made.* New York: Random House, 1999.

Handy, Charles. *The Age of Paradox.* Cambridge: Harvard Business School Press, 1995.

———. "The White Stone: Six Choices." London Business School Alumni News, Spring 1996.

———. *The Age of Unreason.* Cambridge: Harvard Business School Press, 1998.

———. *Beyond Certainty.* Cambridge: Harvard Business School Press, 1998.

———. *The Hungry Spirit.* New York: Broadway Books, 1999.

———. *Waiting for the Mountain to Move.* Hoboken: Jossey-Bass, 1999.

———. *The Elephant and the Flea.*

Cambridge: Harvard Business School Press, 2002.

Hanson, Peter. *The Joy of Stress.* New York: Andrews McMeel Publishing, 1987.

Hauser, Thomas. *Muhammad Ali: His Life and Times.* New York: Simon & Schuster, 1986.

Heller, Joseph. *Closing Time.* New York: Simon & Schuster, 1994.

———. Interview in *Playboy* magazine, June 1975.

Herbert, A. P. *Uncommon Law.* London: Bibliophile, 1984.

Hertsgaard, Mark. *A Day in the Life: The Music and Artistry of the Beatles.* New York: Delacorte Press, 1995.

Hobbs, Michael, ed. *In Celebration of Golf.* New York: Charles Scribner's Sons, 1983.

Horton, Thomas R. *The CEO Paradox.* New York: AMACOM, 1992.

Houston, Jean. *The Possible Human.* Los Angeles: JP Tarcher, 1982.

Huxley, Aldous. *Point Counter Point.* New York: Dalkey, 1996.

Jackson, Phil. *Sacred Hoops.* New York: Hyperion, 1995.

James, Henry. *The Ambassadors.* New York: Chelsea House, 1988.

Jarow, Rick. *Creating the Work You Love.* Rochester: Inner Traditions, 1995.

Jaworski, Joseph. *Synchronicity: The Inner Path of Leadership.* San Francisco: Berrett-Koehler, 1996.

Jeffers, Susan. *Feel the Fear and Do It Anyway.* New York: Fawcett Books, 1992.

Jung, Carl. "The Development of Personality." In *Collected Works,* trans R. F. C. Hull. London: Routledge and Kegan Paul, 1953–79.

———. "The Stages of Life." In *Collected Works,* trans R. F. C. Hull. London: Routledge and Kegan Paul, 1953–79.

———"The Relations between the Ego and the Subconscious." In *Collected Works,* trans R. F. C. Hull. London: Routledge and Kegan Paul, 1953–79.

———. *Memories. Dreams. Reflec-*

tions. New York: Vintage Books, 1989.

———. *Modern Man in Search of a Soul.* New York: Harvest Books, 1955.

Kabat-Zinn, Jon. *Full Catastrophe Living.* New York: Delta, 1990.

———. *Wherever You Go, There You Are.* New York: Hyperion, 1995.

Kennedy, Nigel. *Always Playing.* New York: St Martin's Press, 1992.

Kierkegaard, Søren. *The Sickness Unto Death.* Princeton: Princeton University Press, 1941.

Kornfield, Jack. *A Path with Heart.* New York: Bantam Doubleday Dell, 1993.

———. *After the Ecstasy, the Laundry.* New York: Bantam Doubleday Dell, 2001.

Krishnamurti, J. *The Penguin Krishnamurti Reader.* Harmondsworth: Penguin, 1984.

Kübler-Ross, Elisabeth. *Death—The Final Stage of Growth.* New York: Simon & Schuster, 1986.

Kundera, Milan. *The Unbearable Lightness of Being.* New York: HarperPerennial, 1999.

Kushner, Harold. *When All You've Ever Wanted Isn't Enough.* New York: Fireside, 2002.

Lacey, Robert. *Ford.* New York: Little, Brown, 1992.

Lakein, Alan. *How to Get Control of Your Time and Your Life.* New York: Signet, 1974.

Lama Surya Das. *Awakening the Buddha Within.* New York: Broadway Books, 1997.

Larsen, Stephen and Robin. *A Fire in the Mind: A Life of Joseph Campbell.* New York: Doubleday, 1991.

Larson, Gary. *The Prehistory of the Far Side.* New York: Andrews & McMeel, 1989.

Leakey, Richard. *One Life.* London: Michael Joseph, 1983.

———. *Origins Reconsidered.* New York: Anchor, 1993.

Le Guin, Ursula K. *The Left Hand of Darkness.* New York: Ace Books, 1991.

Leonard, George. *Mastery.* New York: Plume, 1992.

Levine, Stephen. "The Mindful Soul." In *Handbook for the Soul* edited by Richard Carlson and Benjamin Shield. New York: Doubleday, 1996.

Levoy, Gregg. *Callings.* New York: Three Rivers Press, 1998.

Lewis, Sinclair. *Babbitt.* New York: Bantam Classics, 1998.

Liedloff, Jean. *The Continuum Concept.* Cambridge: Perseus Publishing, 1986.

Lindbergh, Anne Morrow. *Gift from the Sea.* New York: Pantheon Press, 1991.

Maddox, Rebecca. *Inc. Your Dreams.* New York: Viking Penguin, 1995.

Mandela, Nelson. *Long Walk to Freedom.* New York: Little, Brown, 1995.

Margolick, David. "On Taking Pity on the Downtrodden Associate." *New York Times,* January 8, 1988.

Mayr, Ernst. *This Is Biology.* Cambridge: Belknap Press, 1998.

Melville, Herman. *Moby-Dick.* New York: Bantam Classics, 1981.

Merton, Thomas. *No Man Is an Island.* New York: Harvest Books, 1978.

Miller, Alice. *The Drama of the Gifted Child.* New York: HarperPerennial, 1997.

Moore, Thomas. *The Re-Enchantment of Everyday Life.* New York: HarperCollins Publishers, 1996.

Moyers, Bill. *Healing and the Mind.* New York: Doubleday, 1993.

Murray, W. H. *The Scottish Himalayan Expedition.* London: Dent, 1951.

Navratilova, Martina. *Martina.* New York: Random House, 1995.

Ornish, Dean. *Dr. Dean Ornish's Program for Reversing Heart Disease.* New York: Ivy Books, 1996.

Pagels, Elaine. *The Origin of Satan.* New York: Random House, 1995.

Paulus, Trina. *Hope for the Flowers.* Mahwah: Paulist Press, 1984.

Peat, F. David. *Blackfoot Physics.* London: Fourth Estate, 1996.

Peck, M. Scott. *The Road Less Traveled.* New York: Touchstone Books, 1998.

———. *Further Along the Road Less Traveled.* New York: Touchstone Books, 1998.

Pert, Candace. "The Chemical Communicators." Interview with Bill Moyers in *Healing and the Mind.* New York: Doubleday, 1993.

Peters, Tom. *Thriving on Chaos.* New York: Alfred A. Knopf, 1987.

———. *Liberation Management.* New York: Alfred A. Knopf, 1992.

Rand, Ayn. *Atlas Shrugged.* New York: New American Library, 1957.

Rechtschaffen, Stephan. *Timeshifting.* New York: Doubleday, 1997.

Rogers, Carl. *On Becoming a Person.* New York: Mariner Books, 1995.

Saul, John Ralston. *Voltaire's Bastards.* New York: Vintage Books, 1993.

Schumacher, E. F. *Good Work.* New York: Harper Colophon, 1980.

Scott, Peter. *The Eye of the Wind.* London: Hodder & Stoughton, 1966.

Selye, Hans. *Stress without Distress.* New York: New American Library, 1975.

Senge, Peter. Introduction to *Synchronicity: The Inner Path of Leadership* by Joseph Jaworski. San Francisco: Berrett-Koehler, 1996.

Shaw, George Bernard. *Man and Superman.* New York: Amereon, 1950.

———. *Shaw on Shakespeare.* New York: Books for Libraries, 1977.

———. *Pygmalion.* New York: Dover, 1994.

Sheehy, Gail. *Passages.* New York: Bantam, 1977.

———. *Understanding Men's Passages.* New York: Random House, 1998.

Sher, Barbara. *I Could Do Anything If Only I Knew What It Was.* New York: Dell, 1995.

Siegel, Bernie. *Living, Loving and Healing.* London: Aquarian, 1993.

———. *Prescriptions for Living.* New York: HarperCollins, 1998.

Sogyal Rinpoche. *The Tibetan Book of Living and Dying.* San Francisco: Harper San Francisco, 1994.

Solomon, Maynard. *Beethoven.* New York: Schirmer Books, 1977.

Stanton, Elizabeth Cady. *Solitude of Self.* Ashfield: Paris Press, 2000.

Steinbeck, John, and Edward Ricketts. *Sea of Cortez.* New York: Paul P. Appel, 1971.

Storr, Anthony. *Churchill's Black Dog.* New York: Ballantine Books, 1990.

Thich Nhat Hanh. *Peace Is Every Step.* New York: Bantam Books, 1991.

Thoreau, Henry David. *Walden.* Boston: Beacon Press, 1998.

Townsend, Robert. *Further Up the Organization.* New York: Random House, 1984.

Vaillant, George E. *Adaptation to Life.* Boston: Little, Brown, 1977.

Vonnegut, Kurt, Jr. *Mother Night.* New York: Dell Publishing, 1986.

Van de Wetering, Janwillem. *The Empty Mirror.* New York: Griffin Trade Paperbacks, 1999.

Wagner, Jane. *The Search for Signs of Intelligent Life in the Universe.* New York: HarperCollins, 1991.

Ward, Timothy. *What the Buddha Never Taught.* Berkeley: Celestial Arts, 1993.

Watts, Alan. *The Wisdom of Insecurity.* New York: Pantheon Books, 1951.

Welch, Jack. *Jack: Straight from the Gut.* New York: Warner Books, 2001.

Wertenbaker, Lael. *The World of Picasso.* New York: Time-Life, 1967.

Wieder, Marcia. *Doing Less and Having More.* New York: William Morris, 1998.

Wilber, Ken. *Grace and Grit.* Boston: Shambhala Publications, 1991.

Wilbur, Richard. "Parable." In *Ceremony and Other Poems.* New York: Harcourt Brace, 1950.

Wolfe, Thomas. *The Web and the Rock.* Baton Rouge: Louisiana State University Press, 1999.

Woodman, Marion. *Conscious Femininity.* Toronto: Inner City Books, 1993.

Wright, Robert. *The Moral Animal.* New York: Vintage Books, 1995.

Zukav, Gary. *The Dancing Wu-Li Masters.* New York: Bantam, 1980.

Index

A Note to Readers

In 1990 I was lucky enough to be taught by Charles Handy at the London Business School. He had us write a reflective paper based on these three questions: Where have I come from? Where am I now? Where am I going?

When I came to the third of those questions, I described perfection: the sort of working life I would ask for if my fairy godmother materialized and granted me one wish. It was appealing, enormously so. But it was also an absurd fantasy. At least, that's how it seemed to me at the time. In fact, I felt a little aggrieved at Charles: it didn't seem fair to embolden me to dream when fulfillment of the dream was impossible.

The paper was soon buried and forgotten. But recently, while cleaning out dusty cartons of yellowed papers, I rediscovered it. I saw then that in the intervening years, my absurd fantasy had become a reality. The impossible dream had come true.

Over the last few years, I've heard many wonderful stories of people who have similarly transformed their lives by adopting the explorer's mind-set and following their bliss. Nearly all have grappled with those inner demons whose message is so insistent: *Get real. Forget about exploring. You have too many family responsibilities. You don't have enough money. You don't have enough talent. You don't have a calling.* Showing grace and grit, patience and courage, humor and resolve, they have persevered and triumphed. You can too.

If you have stories of your own, I would love to hear them. You will find my contact details at **www.themoneyisthegravy.com**

This Web site has tips and resources for bliss-followers. You can also sign up there for my free newsletter.

I wish you well in your exploring. As your journey unfolds, you will find a life—your life. And then you too will have proof that the money *is* just the gravy.

John Clark